# ΛTLΛNTIS

GEOFFREY ASHE

# CONTENTS

# ATLANTIS, the vanished land between Europe and

America, is the noblest setting ever conceived for a drama that has haunted imaginations through the centuries: the drama – the tragedy – of a primordial glory that was lost. It takes many forms, and it interweaves two perennial myths or daydreams, the Golden Age and Ancient Wisdom.

Classical literature is the best-known context for these. Greek poets, such as Hesiod in the 8th century BC, speak of the 'golden race' that flourished before the rise of the present gods. The golden people lived free from care, feeding on the bounty of nature, without disease or decrepitude. They had no government, therefore no misrule; Astraea, goddess of Justice, dwelt among them. Then Zeus (Jupiter in Roman parlance) seized power and the golden world ended. A lesser humanity was taught the arts of life by Prometheus, one of the Titans or elder deities, and Zeus punished him for it.

*The golden people lived free from care, feeding on the bounty of nature, without disease or decrepitude. They had no government, therefore no misrule ...*

Hinduism has its Golden Age in what is known as the Krita Yuga, an age long ago. All creatures were virtuous and wise, fulfilling the inbuilt law of their nature. The Krita Yuga gave way to a series of inferior yugas (ages). Earthly enlightenment began with the Seven Rishis, semi-divine seers or sages, described as 'mysterious beings connected with the origin of humanity and knowledge'. In the *Bhagavad Gita* Krishna, who is the Supreme God incarnate, recalls how he created the Rishis, and himself taught an 'eternal yoga'. But through 'long lapse of time' it was forgotten, and Ancient Wisdom in general decayed with the decline of the world.

➡ A Christian vision of a paradisal world: *The Garden of Earthly Delights*, c. 1500, by Hieronymus Bosch.

Babylonians expressed their view of antiquity by telling of kings living and reigning for thousands of years, and heroes performing superhuman feats. They ascribed civilization's birth to Seven Sages who founded the oldest cities, seemingly the Rishis in Mesopotamian guise. Here too was decline, or at best stagnation. Lives shortened, mortals grew feebler, and the achievements of the Sages were never improved upon.

Judaeo-Christian tradition has its Earthly Paradise or Garden of Eden where unfallen humanity would have dwelt; and Dante, one of the greatest of Christian poets, offers it as the key to even the pagan beliefs. His suggestion is that all Golden Age imaginings, such as those of the Greeks, are rooted in a hazy nostalgia for that lost Paradise. In his *Divine Comedy* its resident Lady says:

> Those men of yore who sang the golden time
> And all its happy state – maybe indeed
> They on Parnassus dreamed of this fair clime.

Nor was it simply a question of innocence and instinctive goodness, repudiated by our first parents. Theologians such as St Thomas Aquinas, whose work Dante knew thoroughly, held that unfallen humans would have been not only far better and happier but also far wiser. Eden's intellectual splendour had no time to unfold, but according to St Thomas, if Adam and Eve had not lost immortality, one of the chief tasks of their indefinitely prolonged years would have been to educate their descendants.

Judaeo-Christian belief recognized that, despite the loss of Paradise, humanity did (so to speak) fight back. Useful arts were developed – agriculture, metallurgy, building – and so were sciences such as astronomy. Yet according to a strong tradition, even these embodied Ancient Wisdom rather than progress, and a supernatural wisdom at that: they were taught by angels who came to earth.

---

← *The Tower of Babel* by Lucas van Valckenborgh, 1594. The Biblical story of the Tower and the myths surrounding it have long been a subject for artists.

Post-Christian minds, retaining the sense of an eclipsed glory, but deprived of doctrinal basis for it, have persisted in picturing lost Golden Ages and Ancient Wisdom. Rousseau did much to inspire the French Revolution with his myth of a long-ago society that was free and equal, and its corruption by elitist civilization. Marxists talked of a classless 'primitive communist' idyll that succumbed to class distinction and exploitation. Away in India, with a Hindu background instead, Mahatma Gandhi created a mass mystique for nationalism out of his vision of a past India of saints and sages and village communes and cottage industry, which alien conquerors had smashed. Well before them, during the European Renaissance, Ancient Wisdom had become a major factor in advanced thinking. Paracelsus and others paid homage to a 'Hermetic' lore said to have been taught in Egypt by the wisdom-god Thoth, and Newton himself thought he was not so much a pioneer as a reviver of Hermetic and kindred knowledge. He believed that writings thousands of years old encoded the Copernican system and gravitation. So it continued, and has continued. Scholars and demi-scholars of later times have found remote origins for practically everything among super-Egyptians or super-Babylonians or super-Druids.

## If Adam and Eve had not lost immortality … one of their chief tasks would have been to educate their descendants.

Yet such hyping-up of known ancient peoples has never carried conviction. The trouble is that they *are* known. In the past century many have preferred to relate the themes to the notion of a huge missing piece of history, a wonderful Something Else far back which is not recognized at present but, once recognized, would put all the past in a new light. The extreme instance is the theory of Erich von Däniken, attributing all human achievement to contact thousands of years ago with higher beings from outer space, and a phase of unequalled creativity under their tutelage. But, more widely and for much longer, such thinking has focused on Atlantis, reflecting a desire to give the drama of glory and loss a local habitation, and causing endless debate as to when-exactly-and-where-exactly.

→ The other side of Eden – hell – depicted in Hieronymus Bosch's triptych *The Garden of Earthly Delights*, c. 1500.

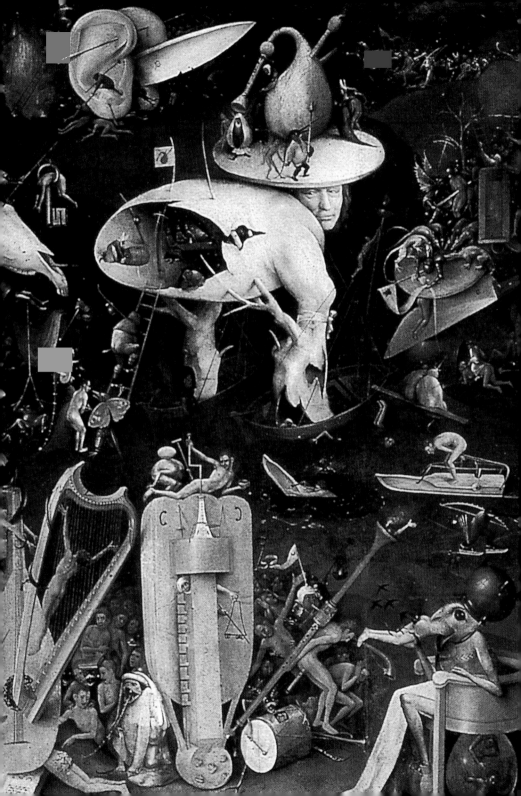

This Atlantean quest has antecedents in the beliefs about Eden, and in medieval guesswork as to its nature and whereabouts. Paradise was lost, yes ... but where had it been? Was it there still, even though mortals could not re-enter? A majority view placed it far to the east (the Bible does say 'east') and very high up. Alexander the Great was said to have reached it in the course of his conquests, but not gone in. Sceptics remarked that neither Alexander nor anyone else had been able to give directions for finding it. To which St Thomas replied:

> The situation of Paradise is shut off from the habitable world by mountains, or seas, or some torrid region, which cannot be crossed; and so people who have written about topography make no mention of it.

Christians who knew the world to be round – as many did – could imagine approaching Paradise by going westward instead of eastward. After all, you would come to the same place. Columbus himself thought it was up the Orinoco. But long before him, some Christians had reflected on paradises lying westward in non-Christian mythology. Homer spoke of the 'Elysian plain at the world's end', where 'no snow falls, no strong winds blow and there is never any rain', and favourites of the gods enjoyed a carefree immortality. Greek legends also pointed to Isles of the Blest or Fortunate Isles, likewise westward across the ocean.

Ireland, too, had a rich Atlantic lore; much richer indeed than the Greek. Irish voyage-romances conjured up an archipelago stretching off into the sunset. Out there lay blessed regions 'without grief, without sorrow, without death', such as Tir na nOg, the Land of Youth, and Mag Mon, a Celtic Elysium itself. Echoing and also promoting beliefs like these, the great Christian voyage-romance of St Brendan the Navigator told of a monk, Barinthus, reaching the borders of Paradise by sailing west, and Brendan himself, inspired by his example, discovering a medley of Atlantic islands and finally attaining the same sanctified territory, in a country of continental extent, after weeks of travel by sea and land.

→ The Mount of Purgatory in Dante's *Divine Comedy*, with the Earthly Paradise at the top. Detail from a fresco in Florence Cathedral, 1465, *Dante and his Poem* by Domenico de Michelino.

Whether or not Dante knew the Brendan story, he too imagined the Earthly Paradise as approachable by sailing west. He placed it on top of a colossal mountain, the Mount of Purgatory, around the other side of a spherical earth. His Mount is on an island in the southern hemisphere, at the antipodes of Jerusalem. In the *Inferno* Ulysses relates how he went westward and southward on his last voyage and came within sight of it, after crossing empty seas for five months. Dante, in the early 14th century, pictures an extended Atlantic with no America in the way.

An idyllic land of harmony among all creatures, pictured as somewhere in America: *The Peaceable Kingdom*. Painting by Thomas Hicks, *c.* 1833.

Dante had his own reasons for implying such a huge distance. Generally, the paradisal land-to-the-west theme did not reach out so far from Europe. But it did reach out, and it persisted. Half a millennium after Dante it was taken up by William Blake in his highly individual poetic mythology. Blake was influenced by eccentric scholars who thought the early Celts of the British Isles, and especially their Druid priesthood, were the source of Ancient Wisdom all over the world. He knew of a legend of early Britain as the domain of 'Albion the giant'. He knew, also, that one of the lands located in what is now the Atlantic was associated with Atlas, the mythical Titan after whom the ocean was named; and it had sunk below the waves. In due course it will be time to ask where this particular tradition came from. Not yet.

Blake identified Atlas with Albion. In the remote past as he portrayed it, Britain, symbolized by Albion-Atlas, was the wellspring of universal enlightenment. During that golden age when a true paradise flourished, humanity was united partly because Albion-Atlas's western territory was above water and formed a link between Britain and America. There, 'Giants dwelt in Intellect'. Albion underwent a 'fall' – Britain's primal sages degenerated, becoming the debased Druids of later history – and one result was that the bridge from Britain to the New World disappeared. Humanity was divided. Yet the land is still there beneath the surface, charged with Titanic energies, which surged up in Blake's own day inspiring the American and French Revolutions.

> On those vast shady hills between America & Albion's shore,
> Now barr'd out by the Atlantic sea, call'd Atlantean hills,
> Because from their bright summits you may pass to the Golden world,
> An ancient palace, archetype of mighty Emperies,
> Rears its immortal pinnacles.

Blake had few readers who came anywhere near to understanding him. But the theme of the lost Atlantic land was spectacularly reborn a few decades later.

# HELENA

Petrovna Blavatsky, HPB as her disciples called her, founded the Theosophical Society in 1875. Born in Russia, she performed as a circus bareback rider, gave piano lessons in London, and travelled to many out-of-the-way places. She was an amusing, magnetic person, very well read, but certainly open to charges of charlatanry and plagiarism.

Her Theosophy did not emerge full-blown at once, but it became (and still is, though it survives more in its influence than in itself) an elaborate system of quasi-religious doctrine and offbeat science. It dealt with cosmic law and reincarnation and the nature of life and innumerable other topics. HPB claimed that she had learned some of its principles from secret writings known only to initiates, and some from Masters of Wisdom or Mahatmas. These were advanced beings who had lived for ages in remote Asian retreats, influencing the world and illuminating a favoured few, by telepathy and other recondite methods.

## Her Theosophy became an elaborate system of quasi-religious doctrine and offbeat science.

Madame Blavatsky's first book was *Isis Unveiled*, published in 1877. Here, among much else, she glanced at the idea of a lost Atlantic land. Without pursuing the topic far, she noted mythic and cultural parallels between the Old World and the New, which pointed, she thought, to a common source in the middle. She was aware also of talk about another lost land, sunk beneath the Indian Ocean. This was a conjecture of scientists, prompted by the belief that the distribution of lemurs and other animals, in Africa and southern Asia, implied a former connection. A geologist, Philip Sclater, had dubbed this bridge Lemuria. In *Isis Unveiled* HPB was non-committal about Lemuria, but interested. She also mentioned theories of a sunken continent in the Pacific, many of the countless islands being remnants of it.

→ Portrait of Helena Petrovna Blavatsky, the founder of the Theosophical Society.

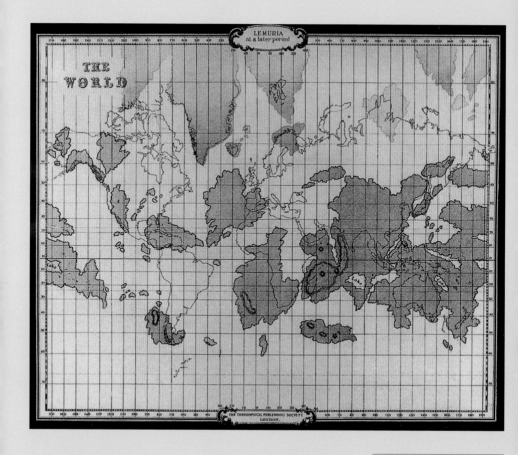

The World

LEMURIA
at a later period

THE THEOSOPHICAL PUBLISHING SOCIETY
LONDON.

A map of Lemuria from 1904. Drawn by Blavatsky devotee William Scott-Elliot in his book *The Lost Lemuria*.

Few outside her Theosophical circle took much notice. But five years later, the Earthly Paradise and Ancient Wisdom and all the rest suddenly reappeared in the midst of the ocean, and a magnificent Atlantis confronted the public. The author who evoked it – versatile, wayward, and, after his fashion, erudite – was, appropriately, of the Celtic stock of Brendan the Navigator.

Ignatius Donnelly was born in Philadelphia, the son of an Irish immigrant. He practised law and was active in politics. Moving to Minnesota, he showed gifts of oratory that brought his election to Congress. He abandoned Washington in 1880 and went back to Minnesota, but his spell in the capital had given him access to the Library of Congress, and his wide reading soon bore fruit.

Scene from the film *Atlantis, the Lost Continent* (1961). This was based partly on Theosophists' accounts of Atlantean magicians in conflict and partly on C. J. Cutcliffe Hyne's 1900 novel *The Lost Continent*, written in the wave of enthusiasm launched by Donnelly, Madame Blavatsky and Scott-Elliot.

Donnelly's *Atlantis: The Antediluvian World* was published in 1882. He declared that a sunken land did exist on the ocean floor. Twelve thousand years ago it was above the surface. It was the true site of Eden, and all earthly paradises in other traditions. It was the home of the world's first civilization, still unsurpassed in spiritual and creative genius. Its people pioneered scientific medicine, the use of metals, alphabetic writing. Their rulers became the gods and goddesses of mythology, Greek, Hindu, Phoenician and Scandinavian. Early civilizations known to history, in Egypt and Mexico and Peru, began as Atlantean offshoots. Atlantis was not the inter-continental bridge imagined by Blake; it was an island, but a very large one, a surviving piece of an even larger land-mass which had partly vanished a long time before. The Atlantean remnant was finally submerged in an upheaval of nature from which few of its people escaped. Accounts of the catastrophe, handed down from those who did, formed the basis of all narratives of a great Flood, biblical and otherwise.

Donnelly took the Blavatsky style of argument enormously further, piling up parallels between the Old World and the New, and drawing inferences about a source in the middle. Thus, mythology on both sides of the ocean supplied Flood legends. It also supplied deities, again on both sides of the ocean, who seemed similar enough to be equated. Study of ancient symbolism revealed (for instance) a pre-Christian reverence for the cross, again on both sides of the ocean. There were pyramids in Egypt and pyramids in Mexico; the prototypes of both were clearly pyramids in Atlantis.

Appraising plant life, Donnelly drew attention to the domestic banana, found in both Africa and America. Botanists said it presupposed a long period of planned cultivation, and where but in Atlantis could this have happened? Linguistics could be invoked too. As Donnelly was aware, philologists had compared Latin, Sanskrit and other languages and inferred an Aryan or Indo-European speech as a common ancestor, far back. It was no great leap to make similar comparisons implying an Atlantean language farther back still, ancestral to many more.

## There were pyramids in Egypt and pyramids in Mexico; the prototypes of both were clearly pyramids in Atlantis.

As we shall see, Donnelly could claim that there was documentary evidence for Atlantis, and he did. But he left it behind; his flamboyant vision was largely his own. It reflected an idealistic outlook. He anticipated H. G. Wells with a novel set in the year 1988, *Caesar's Column*, most of it a condemnation of social trends as he saw them, but ending with a carefully constructed Utopia. His Atlantean arguments had a cumulative impact on many readers; Gladstone was one such, and wanted to send an expedition to examine the sea-bed. Here it all was, in a form that looked scientifically sound – the Golden Age, Ancient Wisdom, the missing piece of history that made sense of the rest. The book was an instant best-seller, even supplying a theme for a New Orleans Mardi Gras carnival, and it has been reprinted dozens of times. Donnelly was elected to the American Association for the Advancement of Science. He had given the lost land a fascination it has possessed ever since.

Meanwhile, Theosophy was not standing still. In *The Secret Doctrine*, published in 1888, Madame Blavatsky had more to say about Atlantis, and Lemuria also. While she cited Donnelly with approval, she was now pressing her claim to knowledge drawn from occult revelations and secret texts. Besides reaffirming Atlantis, she vastly inflated Lemuria, extending it both ways so that it took in the vanished Pacific country and stretched around Africa into the Atlantic. Atlantis itself, she said, was a broken-off portion of it.

➤ The Pyramid of the Sun in Palenque, Mexico, is one of the American parallels with the Old World that are said to point to Atlantis as a common source.

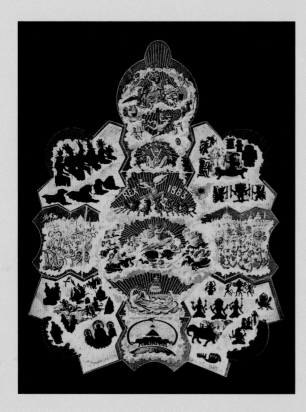

An invitation to a ball in New
Orleans in 1883, when the Mardi
Gras festivities had an Atlantis
theme, inspired by Ignatius
Donnelly's best-selling *Atlantis:
The Antediluvian World*.

→ Easter Island statues, claimed
by some as Lemurian. Engraving from
Comte de La Pérouse's *Relation d'un
Voyage*, 1798.

Her teaching presented an immense panorama of history and prehistory, covering millions of years. She believed that humanity had evolved, but not in a Darwinian sense. Everything of value in Darwin had been familiar to initiates from time immemorial. However, they saw the process differently and knew a great deal which Darwin never dreamed of. One feature of her system, crucial to her thinking about Atlantis and Lemuria, was the way it enabled her to square mythology with scientific fact – or, at any rate, with what she took to be fact. For example, it is an alluring notion that legends of dragons reflect folk-memories of dinosaurs. Palaeontologists reject this on the ground that dinosaurs were extinct before humans appeared. But in Theosophy, humans or proto-humans or quasi-humans existed far enough back to overlap with the dinosaurs. Therefore dragon legends make perfectly good, literal sense. In the same spirit HPB could checkmate any geologist who denied the submergence of inhabited land in the Atlantic because such submergence, if it happened at all, would have been too long ago for the land to be inhabited. Theosophical humankind – of some sort – was old enough to be contemporary.

Her redrawn map of Earth in antiquity was the stage for her saga of human evolution, and closely related to its phases. She envisaged a series of seven 'root-races' in a series of continents, over aeons of time. The first root-race, astral and invisible, lived in an Imperishable Sacred Land which she left nebulous. Second were the Hyperboreans, slightly more like people as now understood, in a continent that comprised northern Asia and parts of the Arctic. Third came the inhabitants of Lemuria. They were huge and hermaphroditic. Some had four arms, and eyes at the back of their heads. Yet they were a further step towards familiar humanity, and their era was reasonably happy. Lemuria, however, sank.

Atlantis entered as the home of the fourth root-race. The Atlanteans were still tall, but definitely like ourselves, male and female, and highly civilized, the founders of civilizations known to history. On that point, said HPB, Donnelly was right. They also founded orders of wise men such as the Druids and Brahmins. Atlantis also sank. The fifth and currently predominant race is the Aryan, with its main achievements in Europe. North America is evolving the sixth race, and South America will perhaps evolve the seventh.

HPB's use of such words as 'race' and 'Aryan' may suggest attitudes now condemned. While the condemnation would fit some of her followers, it is less than fair applied to herself. She was thinking not so much of ethnic groups or blood-kinships as of phases of development, mental and physical. Moreover, she divided each of her races into sub-races widely different from each other. The world's present population, though dominated by the race she calls Aryan, is made out to be a mélange including many descendants of the previous ones.

Some of the most exciting passages in HPB's *The Secret Doctrine* were those concerning the lost lands. Her hints were expanded after her death by William Scott-Elliot, a merchant banker and amateur anthropologist. His books *The Story of Atlantis* (1896) and *The Lost Lemuria* (1904) won the guarded approval of the Theosophical Society. Though not lacking conventional scholarship, Scott-Elliot relied mainly on 'astral clairvoyance'.

## The Atlanteans were still tall, but definitely like ourselves, male and female, and highly civilized, the founders of civilizations known to history.

He claimed that the world's surface had been changed by several upheavals over the past million years or so. Partly because of his disclosures, the bias of Lemuria, in occult teaching, shifted to the Pacific. Reaching backward beyond his million years, he revealed Lemurians twelve feet tall, leading tame plesiosaurs on leashes. Despite this feat of domestication, they were not an advanced people. Lemuria was destroyed by volcanic action. Before that, however, higher beings from Venus had arrived as teachers of useful arts, such as metallurgy, agriculture, and large-scale building.

→ Shown here in an engraving entitled *The Secret of Immortality* is Androgyne, a human who transcends sexual polarity, rising out of the sea. Image illustrating Georgi Golokhvastov's 1938 poem 'Gibel' Atlantidy' ('The Fall of Atlantis').

According to Scott-Elliot, descendants of the Lemurians can still be identified. Some are primitive: Australian aborigines, African bushmen. Chinese, however, is a Lemurian-derived language. The Atlanteans evolved from the best Lemurian elements. Their sub-races included the original Semites and Mongols. But Atlantis's chief sub-race was the Toltec, a term applied in conventional history to the builders of Tula north of Mexico City.

The gifted Toltecs were eight feet tall and had a magnificent capital, the City of the Golden Gates, which is now under the sea, west of Senegal. Their civilization was very splendid and very knowledgeable. They expanded into America, Egypt and Britain, building pyramids and Stonehenge. (The occultist Dion Fortune, following up some of Scott-Elliot's revelations, claimed that Somerset was an Atlantean colony and that Brent Knoll, near the Bristol Channel, was a pyramid – or anyhow, a hill artificially shaped by the colonists.) The Toltecs had aircraft using a kind of jet propulsion, limited in power, so that aviators could not fly over hills of any height but had to go round. They practised magic, and, for a long time, applied their psychic and paranormal techniques benignly. But some took to sorcery for selfish and evil ends. This led to an inundation followed by further disasters, culminating in the final debacle. The fall of Atlantis was essentially a moral fall.

## The gifted Toltecs were eight feet tall and had a magnificent capital, the City of the Golden Gates, which is now under the sea.

← Toltec statues from the Post-Classical period at Tula, Mexico. William Scott-Elliot's Toltecs were the standard-bearers of Atlantean civilization in America, Egypt and Britain, and had psychic and paranormal powers. The statues at Tula are, however, far more recent than his Atlantis.

Thus far William Scott-Elliot. Rudolf Steiner, who started out among the Theosophists and then moved off on his own, had his say about Atlantis but did not add very much. One of the ablest members of his circle was Dimitri Merezhkovsky (1865–1941), a Russian historical novelist of some note, whose *Atlantis/Europe: The Secret of the West* appeared under Steinerite auspices. Merezhkovsky is closer to Donnelly than to the occultists. For him too, Atlantis was the locale of the Earthly Paradise. It was also the Avalon of Arthurian legend. Its civilization was the source of others and 'the seed of Europe'. Merezhkovsky traces connections with known mythologies, identifying Atlas, the lost land's original overlord, with the biblical Enoch. Seven Atlantean gods, he thinks, survived the disaster and found their way into later pantheons: Adonis, Osiris, Tammuz, Attis, Mithra, Dionysus, and Quetzalcoatl. He also foreshadows the ideas of some feminist prehistorians concerning an ancient, eclipsed goddess-worship and the need for its reinstatement.

# THEOSOPHISTS linked their vanished

continents with Buddhist beliefs. By casting the net wider, they drew in an established Asian paradise which no ingenuity could have placed in the Atlantic or the Pacific. Tibetan and Mongolian lamas tell of Shambhala, an earthly point of contact with spiritual realms. Westerners have made guesses about it with too little attention to what is actually said, locating it, for instance, in the Himalayas – whence James Hilton's Shangri-la. The lamas are clear that Shambhala is in the north, and various indications point towards the Altai Mountains. In this hidden place Buddha himself underwent initiation; the epic hero Gesar, a sort of Arthur, vanished into it and will some day return; it has semi-divine kings, who embody a god and influence the world telepathically, and one of whom will emerge as a Messiah.

## Shambhala is in the north, and various indications point towards the Altai Mountains. In this hidden place Buddha himself underwent initiation

Madame Blavatsky did not know much about the tradition, and was not deeply concerned with it, but she fitted it in. *The Secret Doctrine* quotes a passage said to be from an ancient book, stating that some 'elect' Lemurians took refuge in a sacred island which 'is now the "fabled" Shamballah, in the Gobi Desert'. The Gobi Desert was then a lake.

➤ A 19th-century Mongolian mandala of the kingdom of Shambhala. Here, the king is in the mountainous north where Shambhala lies hidden from ordinary mortals, who can only go there if summoned.

An east-Tibetan Tanka of Gesar, the principal hero of Tibetan and Mongolian epic, who is said to be still living in Shambhala and destined to reappear.

*Opposite | Treasure of the World – Chintamani* (1924) by Nicholas Roerich. The treasure is a sacred stone bearing divine fire, which the horse is bringing down from the mountains to illuminate the world. The image is related to Shambhala's destined inauguration of a new era.

The Shambhalic hint was taken up by Nicholas Roerich, the distinguished Russian artist who supplied anthropological material for Stravinsky's *Rite of Spring*. Roerich was a Theosophist for a while, and, during an expedition through Central Asia in the 1920s, learned more about Shambhala than HPB ever did. He brought to light many facts of interest, but dismissed or ignored the specific Theosophical aspect, the connection with Lemuria. This was developed, or rather rethought, in the breakaway school of Alice Bailey, whose teachings were popularized in the 1930s by Vera Stanley Alder.

The Bailey-Alder 'Shamballa' (as they spell it) was founded by higher beings from Venus eighteen million years ago, a detail adapted from Scott-Elliot. It was on the Gobi island. Its principal human phase involved Atlanteans. On the south shore of the Gobi lake, about 60,000 BC, they founded a settlement that became the cradle of the fifth, or Aryan, root-race. The settlement grew into a city, Manova, the City of the Bridge, so named from a bridge over the lake joining it with Shamballa. Manova was at its zenith about 45,000 BC. Shamballa is still there in the desert, but imperceptible. It is the earthly home of the spiritual Hierarchy – Blavatsky's Masters – who meet there annually.

# THOUGH

Atlantis was installed in the occult scheme of things, it kept a character in its own right independent of occultism. Donnelly and others were exponents of a 'serious' Atlantis tradition. Lemuria was less tangible. Defunct as a Victorian geological theory, it survived mainly, in an expanded form, through Madame Blavatsky and Scott-Elliot. For a long time attempts to substantiate it in Donnelly's manner were few, and the only one to attract much attention was still an outgrowth of ideas about 'cosmic forces'. Its author was James Churchward, a British army officer, and he set up, in effect, as a rival to Donnelly.

*Brasseur de Bourbourg, who thought he had deciphered a Maya script, 'translated' an account of a volcanic cataclysm that wrecked Mu. The first believers in his decipherment equated Mu with Atlantis.*

Churchward drew inspiration from studies of the Maya of Yucatan. Brasseur de Bourbourg, a scholar who thought he had deciphered the Maya script, 'translated' an account of a volcanic cataclysm that wrecked a country called Mu. The first believers in his decipherment equated Mu with Atlantis. Churchward dissented. Mu was the real name of Lemuria, conceived now as in the Pacific only. It extended 6,000 miles from east to west, 3,000 from north to south. Easter Island, with its bizarre statues, was a surviving fragment. Churchward claimed for Mu the sort of exalted attributes others had claimed for Atlantis. It contained the Garden of Eden, and it had 'the highest and most ancient civilization the world has known'. According to Churchward's own account, a Hindu priest taught him an almost-forgotten language, Naacal, enabling him to translate a series of stone tablets that gave him the history of Mu. Travelling widely, he collected symbols, myths and folklore from all sides, giving Muvian interpretations.

→ An eruption on the island of Surtsey off Iceland in 1963. Volcanic activity in this part of the world has been observed for a long time. Sometimes it has had tangible geographic effects, with islets changing shape, appearing, and disappearing. Advocates of a literal fall of Atlantis have collected Icelandic instances in support of its possibility.

Mu, or Lemuria, may look more plausible than Atlantis. Surely those many Pacific islands could be the high points of a land-mass that once united them and afterwards sank, but not completely? Geologically this is said not to work. Lemuria, however, has continued to have its advocates, though without Churchward's implied anti-Atlantean stance. An important though delayed influence has been a book published in 1894 – before Churchward – entitled *A Dweller on Two Planets*.

## A belief which grew up was that a select group of Lemurians retired into Mount Shasta's interior. Their descendants are still there and occasionally emerge.

On the face of it this is a novel, its author Frederick Spencer Oliver. But Oliver explained that it had been transmitted by 'Phylos the Thibetan', much of it within sight of Mount Shasta in northern California. While most of the story takes place in a Utopian Atlantis, Oliver introduces Lemuria too, though not at much length. He speaks of an artificial chamber inside Mount Shasta. Some of his readers took the view that he was an inspired being with a long series of incarnations, one of them as Lemuria's emperor. A belief which grew up was that a select group of Lemurians retired into Mount Shasta's interior. Their descendants are still there and occasionally emerge. In 1936 a Lemurian Fellowship was formed, and developed the topic of Shasta's underground temple, which was now enlarged into a system of chambers at the end of a passage, behind a great stone door. A ramification of this belief was that the American Pacific states were once actually part of Lemuria, stayed above water when it sank, and became attached to a different continent.

A Lemuria-related Shasta mystique endures. In 1987 the Harmonic Convergence, a New Age event focused on reputed energy-centres, drew several thousands to the mountain. Two years later a group of artists in the area published an anthology of their work, with the title *The New Visionaries* and the sub-title 'from Mt. Shasta (with love)'.

Shasta has authentic status in Native American myth. Donnelly knew this, and summarized the chief myth in one of his later books, which Oliver may or may not have known. It tells of the origin of the world and the beginning of humankind. The Great Spirit created Shasta first of all things, and built the rest around it. He is still in a chamber inside. Though Oliver may have picked up this notion of a hollow and inhabited mountain, the Shasta-Lemuria mystique does not seem to have much connection with genuine Native American motifs. Exceptional here, it is right to add, is one of the visionary artists, Cheryl Yambrach Rose. Having studied certain pictographs and petroglyphs, she judges that these are proofs of an unidentified senior culture which can be interpreted as Lemurian.

Mount Shasta, the fifth highest peak in California, is over 4,300 metres high (14,100 ft) and remains the focus of New Age attention today.

# OCCULT

teachings had their impact on novelists. Edgar Rice Burroughs, best known as the inventor of Tarzan, made his début in 1912 with a magazine serial set on the planet Mars. It was published in book form, and several more followed. The chief character, John Carter, is wafted back and forth between worlds by a kind of paranormal travel such as Theosophists have ascribed to Tibetan lamas. At first his flights simply happen, afterwards he learns to control them. Burroughs's descriptions of Mars are based partly on the theories of Percival Lowell, an astronomer who thought the lines on its surface were straight and formed a network, and inferred that they were irrigation canals dug by Martians to make optimum use of scanty water. Lowell had no specific image of his canal-diggers. Burroughs imagined two main intelligent species, co-existing: gigantic green Martians with several arms, and noble red Martians who were human, though with biological differences that didn't show. The former were like Blavatsky's Lemurians, the latter like the chief Atlantean sub-race, the Toltecs, even using rather feeble flying-machines. Burroughs glanced at Atlantis more directly in an African tale, *Tarzan and the Jewels of Opar* (1918).

*The moon preceding our own dragged the seas up and up, so that the civilizations of the time developed in high places ...*

Arthur Conan Doyle, like Burroughs, is best remembered as the creator of a fictional character, Sherlock Holmes. But he too was wide-ranging. His late novel *The Maracot Deep* (1928) is a curious hybrid. Up to a point it is science-fiction, telling of a descent into the ocean. An Atlantean city, enclosed and flourishing, is found on the sea-bed. The last part of the story echoes Scott-Elliot with his evil magicians. Conan Doyle was never a Theosophist. The ruling interest of his last years was Spiritualism. It may, at least, have disposed him to respect the kind of communication Scott-Elliot claimed.

→ Cover illustration by Frank R. Paul for the fantasy magazine *Wonder Stories* (February 1935). Sci-fi stories such as Nathaniel Salisbury's story *The Moon Doom* have been influenced by stories of Atlantis. He imagines New York succumbing to tides, as Atlantis was said to have.

WONDER Stories

HUGO GERNSBACK
Editor

A GERNSBACK PUBLICATION

"THE MOON DOOM"

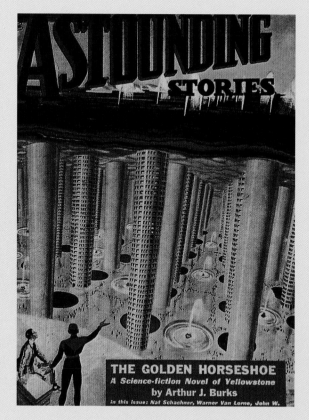

Flights of speculation in fiction and out of it bred further notions about Atlantis, some related directly to Theosophy, some only in the sense that Theosophy promoted the sort of thinking that underlay them. Lost continents had a place in the cosmology of Hans Höbiger, which was fashionable in Nazi Germany. Among much else he asserted that Earth has had at least four moons, but only one at a time, because in each case the orbit decayed so that the satellite spiralled inwards, broke up, and fell in fragments. The series of moons played a crucial role in geological changes and the evolution of life. When they were close, their upward gravitational pull produced large creatures below: dinosaurs, for instance. The moon preceding our own dragged the seas up and up, so that the civilizations of the time developed in high places, such as Tiahuanaco in the Andean Altiplano. These civilizations included a first Atlantis. As the moon drew nearer it caused natural catastrophes that ruined them. Its fragments finally struck, 150,000 years ago, after which the super-tides ceased and the waters settled, but the first Atlantis was gone. The second Atlantis was substantially Donnelly's, containing the true Earthly Paradise, and spreading its impressive culture widely. When Earth captured its present moon, 12,000 years ago, tidal waves and floods overwhelmed the second Atlantis and also Lemuria. Humanity declined, but Atlantis had planted seeds of civilization in Egypt and elsewhere. Höbiger's lunar notions were developed in England by H. S. Bellamy, author of *Moons, Myths, and Man* (1936).

A real Atlantis or Neo-Atlantis, in the depths, is a UFO base now run by alien astronauts, who bring surface-dwellers down, train them, and send them back above for their own purposes.

Another radical belief introducing Atlantis is the Hollow Earth theory. It has taken several forms. According to the most thoroughgoing we inhabit a fairly thin shell enclosing a vast spherical space, lit from within by a miniature sun or suns. One or two 18th-century scientists speculated on these lines, and in 1818 Captain John Symmes developed the idea. Jules Verne mentions it in *A Journey to the Centre of the Earth*, though even in a novel that demands interior spaces he does not go all the way with it. Edgar Rice Burroughs, in *At the Earth's Core*, does go all the way, imagining a world called Pellucidar on the inner surface living in the perpetual day of a central fire.

Enthusiasts have maintained that there is a way in via the North Pole, and perhaps another via the South Pole. Modified versions such as Verne's reduce the internal space, but still give room for subterranean peoples. The Victorian novelist Edward Bulwer-Lytton, who had esoteric interests, invented such a people in *The Coming Race*, which many thought was a coded presentation of fact. At any rate, some say Atlanteans and Lemurians got into the interior and are still there; and some say it is from this same interior that Unidentified Flying Objects enter the atmosphere. It has been suggested that a real Atlantis or Neo-Atlantis, in the depths, is a UFO base now run by alien astronauts, who bring surface-dwellers down, train them, and send them back above for their own purposes.

BEHIND many Atlantean speculations, sober and otherwise, is a wish to believe not only in a glory that *was* but in a glory that in some way still *is*. The Golden Age, the Ancient Wisdom, existed once and were lost ... but no, they were not truly lost. Atlantis can return. It is like King Arthur, undying in Avalon, or asleep in a cave, or, at the very least, inspiring the generations after him with an immortal legend. Atlantis survives through its influence, if no more; and since it has hitherto been a missing piece of history, its recognition and rediscovery can make the world look different. The bolder speculators go further. Atlanteans exist still and signal their presence by means of ... well, UFOs, for instance. Or the world harbours caches of Atlantean secrets that will one day be revealed.

Colin Amery, author of *New Atlantis* (1976), believes in a Hall of Records near the Sphinx, in Egypt. His main reasons are paranormal. One of his precursors is H. C. Randall-Stevens, who predicted, on the authority of an 'Osirian' group, that Atlantis will resurface in 2014 and the Great Pyramid will yield up a body of lost knowledge. His other precursor is Edgar Cayce, famous as the Sleeping Prophet.

## H. C. Randall-Stevens predicted that Atlantis will resurface in 2014 and the Great Pyramid will yield up a body of lost knowledge ...

Born on a Kentucky farm in 1877, Cayce began, in his twenties, to go into self-induced trances in which he diagnosed people's illnesses and prescribed cures, often unorthodox but with a high success rate. He went on to give 'readings' of wider scope. Awake, he was a straightforward Bible Christian, and he was disturbed to learn that in his trances he was telling people of their past lives and thereby endorsing reincarnation. Later he succeeded in reconciling his revelations with Christian doctrine. They included a good deal about Atlantis. He gave accounts of a technologically advanced society, with aircraft, electricity, and a power source vaguely suggesting atomic energy – not yet released in Cayce's time, but foreseen. Atlantis's end came through a combination of natural disaster and misuse of applied science – a variant of Scott-Elliot's moral fall.

Cayce foretold the discovery of a sealed chamber near the Sphinx containing Atlantis's history. He also foretold that in the late 1960s the western part of the lost land would begin to reappear in the Bahamas. In 1968 (twenty-three years after Cayce's death) divers reported, near the Bahamian island of Andros, what looked like a ruined building on the sea-bed. Claims were also made about a paved road under the water near Bimini. Both, however, may have been natural formations.

# SUCH

is the Atlantis mythos of modern times. It has two remarkable features.

First, Ignatius Donnelly built his case around the work of a Greek author more than two thousand years earlier: an author who mystifies, tantalizes, and evokes a feeling of authenticity that has made Atlantis carry conviction in spite of all fantasy, and persuaded less ardent spirits than Donnelly to believe in it.

A marble bust of Plato dating from the 1st century BC.

→ Plato's Academy, the group in which his Atlantis story took shape. Mosaic from a villa near Pompeii, before AD 79.

Secondly, whatever that author believed himself, he meant his story to have a mythic dimension and make a statement about the human condition. But his followers, from Donnelly onward, have shifted the focus and changed the meaning. However retold, the story has become a different story.

Atlantis makes its first appearance in the writings of the philosopher Plato. He lived from about 427 to 347 BC, mainly in Athens, and was the principal disciple of Socrates, whom he knew in late middle age when he himself was in his twenties. Plato's writings take the form of imaginary conversations known as dialogues. Socrates is the star speaker, talking with members of his circle. How far Plato is presenting him as he was, how far making him a mouthpiece for ideas of his own, is a difficult question. The mouthpiece aspect certainly grew more conspicuous as Plato went on writing and the real Socrates faded into the past. The passages about Atlantis are probably almost pure Plato. They occur in two of the dialogues, *Timaeus* and *Critias*.

*These histories tell of a mighty power which unprovoked made an expedition against the whole of Europe and Asia …*

Critias, a senior relative of Plato himself, speaks in *Timaeus* of a story handed down in his family. His great-grandfather heard it from Solon, the Athenian lawgiver. During the first half of the 6th century BC Solon visited Saïs in Egypt and discussed Greek legends and traditions with a priest of the goddess Neith. The priest remarked that Egyptians knew of an event highly creditable to Athens which the Athenians themselves did not. Nine thousand years ago, he said, Athens was a republic with an honourable record of good government and public achievement. It perished, and millennia were to pass before its rebirth, but its last phase was heroic and tragic.

Many great and wonderful deeds are recorded of your state in our histories. But one of them exceeds all the rest in greatness and valour. For these histories tell of a mighty power which unprovoked made an expedition against the whole of Europe and Asia, and to which your city put an end. This power came forth out of the Atlantic Ocean, for in those days the Atlantic was navigable; and there was an island situated in front of the straits which are by you called the pillars of Heracles [Gibraltar]; the island was larger than Libya and Asia put together, and was the way to other islands, and from these you might pass to the whole of the opposite continent which surrounded the true ocean; for this sea which is within the Straits of Heracles [the Mediterranean] is only a harbour, having a narrow entrance; but that other is a real sea, and the land surrounding it on every side may be most truly called a boundless continent.

Now in this island of Atlantis there was a great and wonderful empire which had rule over the whole island and several others, and over parts of the continent, and furthermore, the men of Atlantis had subjected the parts of Libya within the columns of Heracles as far as Egypt, and of Europe as far as Tyrrhenia [Etruria in north Italy]. This vast power, gathered into one, endeavoured to subdue at a blow our country and yours and the whole of the region within the straits; and then, Solon, your country shone forth, in the excellence of her virtue and strength, among all mankind. She was pre-eminent in courage and military skill, and was the leader of the Hellenes. And when the rest fell off from her, being compelled to stand alone, after having undergone the very extremity of dangers, she defeated and triumphed over the invaders, and preserved from slavery those who were not yet subjugated, and generously liberated all the rest of us who dwelt within the pillars.

*The Fall of the Giants*, 1532–34, by Giulio Romano, Mantua, Italy. Giants built a colossal pyramid of rocks in an attempt to scale the heavens.

Poseidon, the Greek god of Atlantis. Silver stater from Poseidonia (Paestum), c. 510 BC.

But afterwards there occurred violent earthquakes and floods; and in a single day and night of misfortune all your warlike men in a body sank into the earth, and the island of Atlantis in like manner disappeared into the depths of the sea. For which reason the sea in those parts is impassable and impenetrable, because there is a shoal of mud in the way; and this was caused by the subsidence of the island.'

Solon, who was a poet as well as a legislator, was so much impressed by what the Egyptian told him that he planned to make it the theme of an epic, and possibly composed some of this, but never finished.

How big was Atlantis? Larger than Libya and Asia put together. 'Libya' means North Africa, but there is no indication how much of it. 'Asia' as the term is used here would mean a portion of the continent extending from Asia Minor into Arabia and Iran. Atlantis would thus have been bigger than Australia, perhaps considerably bigger. A further geographical point is arresting, more so now than in Plato's day, the allusion to islands beyond and a 'boundless continent' with Atlantean colonies in it. America?

Plato expands Critias's account in the dialogue named after him. This fuller version ostensibly makes use of a manuscript by Solon, which Critias's forebears acquired and kept. While a Utopian Athens figures again, in some detail, much is made of Atlantis as a kind of Utopia itself, but in the end a failed and perverted one. The passage is an elaborate prologue to the war and cataclysm sketched in *Timaeus*.

*The Farnese Atlas*, 1st or 2nd century AD. Atlas, reputedly Poseidon's son, was the first king of the island of Atlantis.

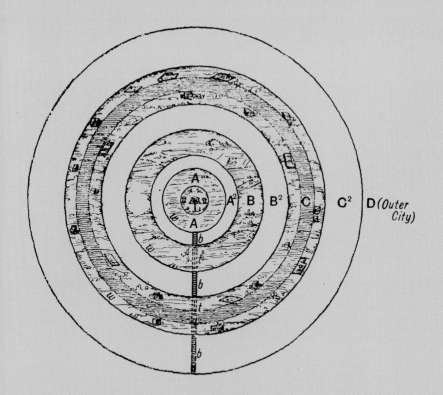

A  A²  B  B²  C  C²  D *(Outer City)*

In *Critias* we learn that the island took its name from the Titan
Atlas, as did the Atlas Mountains in Morocco and the neighbouring
ocean. It was Atlas's Isle. In Greek myth he is one of the deities who
ruled before the rise of Zeus. Critias, however, makes out that he was
junior rather than senior. The narrative begins with Zeus's brother
Poseidon (Neptune) taking possession of the island, as yet unnamed.
It had human inhabitants, among them a couple with a daughter, Cleito.
They lived on a hill near the coast. Cleito's parents died and Poseidon
cohabited with her. They had ten sons, Atlas being the first-born. The
rulers of Atlantis, henceforth known by that name, were all descended
from these. The island was divided into ten portions, each governed by
its own king. In the course of time the kings' power extended to other
islands and into Europe and Africa. The one in the direct line from Atlas
was always paramount. His territory included the hill where Cleito
had lived, and his palace was on it. Poseidon had isolated this hill by
surrounding it with three broad concentric rings of water; the whole
system was just under 5 kilometres (3 miles) across.

Atlantis's royal inner
city; a modern plan
(1929) illustrating
Plato's description.
The hill of Cleito in the
centre is surrounded by
three moats.

A more recent interpretation of
Atlantis's capital: *Atlantis* by Peter
Connolly, 1990. The rings of water
and the bridges echo Plato's account
of the city.

Atlantis, enjoying internal peace through harmony
among its rulers, grew populous and wealthy. It was well
provided with animals, notably elephants, and with forests,
vegetation in general, and minerals. It had two harvests a year.
The Atlanteans set a high value on a metal called orichalcum,
which was a copper alloy, though it is spoken of here as if it
were a precious metal in its own right. The royal hill of Cleito
became a citadel around which a metropolis grew. Poseidon's
concentric moats were bridged, and converted into harbours,
with connecting underpasses and a canal to the sea. The rings
of land between them, and the central hill, had walls around
their perimeters, the outermost being plated with bronze,
the next with tin, the innermost with orichalcum. On the hill
itself, besides the palace, there stood a temple dedicated to
Poseidon and Cleito, covered with silver. Its floor and interior
walls were of orichalcum, its ceiling of ivory, its pinnacles
of gold. Close by, thanks to the god's foresight in providing
springs, were fountains and warm baths. One of the girdling
rings of land had a racecourse on it.

Outside the whole complex were commercial and residential quarters, and beyond was a vast plain, still within the paramount kingdom. About 300 miles long and 200 wide, it was parcelled out into 60,000 equal sections, each with a 'leader'. Among other responsibilities, he had to recruit soldiers for any overseas war. The king's armed forces included thousands of horse-drawn chariots and a navy. The plain was kept fertile by irrigation canals. Much of the rest of Atlantis was high ground, with coastal ranges and precipices.

*For many generations the rulers retained a touch of their divine ancestry, and governed as enlightened despots ... But at last the divine spark faded and ... they became prey to unrighteous ambition ...*

All ten regional rulers had absolute powers, but were bound by a constitutional code handed down from Poseidon and inscribed on a pillar of orichalcum in his temple. There they assembled for consultations at intervals of five and six years alternately. They opened the proceedings with the sacrifice of a bull. Its blood ran down the pillar and they swore to uphold the constitution. After this ritual they held their conference at night, wearing blue robes. In effect Atlantis was a loose federation, and, as noted in *Timaeus*, it could be 'gathered into one' to act as a whole.

A vision of Atlantis's royal palace: a set design by Sir Gerald Hargreaves for his 'fantasy with music' *Atalanta* (*c.* 1950). This is one of the few modern treatments to retain Plato's story of an attempt by Atlantis to conquer Athens.

For many generations the rulers retained a touch of their divine ancestry, and governed as enlightened despots, with wisdom and moderation. But at last the divine spark faded, and although they appeared as splendid as ever, they became prey to unrighteous ambition and power-hunger. Hence the phase of over-extended imperialism that eventually led to the ruin already sketched. They were inviting retribution at the hands of Zeus, now supreme over the universe, and he responded. Summoning the rest of the gods he began to speak. ...

At which point the narrative breaks off. *Critias* is unfinished, though it has been made clear several pages back what the doom of Atlantis is going to be – the same as in *Timaeus* – and that the heroic Athenians are to perish in the disaster with their opponents.

# RESPONSES AND INTERPRETATIONS

THIS then is where it came from, this is what Donnelly and the rest wove their fabrics around. Donnelly believed Plato's story to be true, though only as part of the more grandiose truth which he inferred on other grounds. A word of clarification is called for. Modern authors have sometimes assumed that Greeks and Egyptians had a recognized Atlantis tradition, and that Plato simply gives us the fullest report of it. That may be so, but there is no solid evidence. Plato is not merely the leading witness, he is virtually the only one. In the 1st century AD another Greek, Plutarch, mentions Solon's poetic project, but is probably only copying Plato. Robert Graves in his *Greek Myths* theorizes that the dramatist Thespis, with whom Solon quarrelled, retorted with a skit parodying talk of Atlantis on the lawgiver's part. This would be proof that Solon did talk of it, but not a line of the hypothetical skit survives.

If there was a broader tradition we would expect to find other Greeks mentioning it and accepting Plato's story as factual. In spite of his great prestige, this hardly ever happens. His own chief disciple, Aristotle, thought he made Atlantis up. Crantor, who edited *Timaeus* about 300 BC, did believe in Atlantis, but seemingly on Plato's word only, not because he had outside knowledge. Other classical authors who refer to it very seldom enlarge on it or commit themselves in favour. A nation called the Atlantes, whom Greek historians do recognize, were Africans living near Mount Atlas and the Atlantic Ocean, not inhabitants of the lost land.

Yet Plato's story is so detailed and circumstantial that quite a number of readers, even before the modern interest, found it hard to dismiss totally. When America was discovered, or rediscovered, some concluded that here was the real Atlantis – that is, the land Plato was really talking about. It was still there, of course, but maybe the ancients had lost whatever contact they had with it, and supposed it to have sunk. Those who took this view ignored Plato's distinction between Atlantis and the continent on the far side, which would be his

→ The location of the sunken island Atlantis according to the Egyptians' and Plato's description. Map from *Mundus subterraneus* by Athanasius Kircher, 1664.

*Insula Atlantis.*

America if anything was. Their equation was helped by news that the Aztecs of Mexico spoke of an ancestral homeland called Aztlan, presumably somewhere in the New World. Richard Hakluyt, the Elizabethan compiler of books on voyages, was inclined to accept America as Atlantis. Some explorers cherished a hope that part of it *had* been submerged, opening a North–West passage to the Orient. 'Atlantis' was proposed as a name for the New World before 'America' was finally settled on. America is poetically 'Atlantis' for Shelley, and the 'New Atlantis' in Anatole France's satire *Penguin Island* (1909).

Francis Bacon, however, coined the term 'New Atlantis' long before, early in the 17th century. With More's *Utopia* in mind, he invented another Utopia himself, an island in the Pacific. This for him was the New Atlantis because America itself was the old one. Thousands of years ago America's chief kingdoms were Mexico and Peru. It was the Mexicans whose fleet entered the Mediterranean, and who attempted the Platonic conquest in that part of the world. Their expedition never returned, doubtless owing to the defeat of which Solon's Egyptian priest heard a confused account. The Peruvians sailed west and reached the New Atlantis, called Bensalem by its inhabitants. America, Old Atlantis, was overwhelmed by a devastating flood that thinned the population and reduced most of it to savagery.

William Blake has already been mentioned. There is no telling whether he believed in Atlantis as a literal fact; he may have regarded 'fact' as irrelevant or unimportant.

In the days of these literary rehandlers, anyone who thought of Atlantis at all was likely either to dismiss it as fiction or, as in the American theory, explain it away. A few suspected otherwise, such as the Jesuit scholar Athanasius Kircher, and a further few tried to relocate it. The archives of geography include conjectural maps. But the explosion of literal belief came only in the latter part of the 19th century. Jules Verne – of whom more in due course – supplied a hint. The ground was prepared also by the discovery of the Mid-Atlantic Ridge, a submerged mountain range running roughly north and south, and breaking surface in the Azores. Helena Petrovna Blavatsky spoke up in 1877; Ignatius Donnelly in 1882; Madame Blavatsky again in 1888.

---

◄ Portrait of Thomas More, the author of *Utopia*, from 1527.

# THE ROUGH ROAD TO ATLANTOLOGY

**IT** was Donnelly who built a non-occult, 'rational' Atlantis on Plato's foundation, though, even as such, its mythic power was plain. Despite the huge success of his book, it was some time before the subject was carried further along his own quasi-scientific line. Critical scrutiny of his arguments, and those of his followers, gradually revealed the problems Plato had bequeathed.

Augustus le Plongeon, a pioneer excavator of sites in Yucatan, tried to connect the Maya script with Egyptian hieroglyphics. Relying on Brasseur de Bourbourg's decipherment, he claimed that a Maya codex told of the destruction of Mu, and that Mu was Atlantis. He produced a romantic tale, versified in 1902 by his wife, about an Atlantean queen named Moo who went to Egypt, became the goddess Isis, and founded Egyptian civilization: a filling-in of Donnelly's theory on the birth of Egypt. Le Plongeon's lost land was the Mu afterwards adopted by Churchward and transferred to the Pacific as a redrawn Lemuria. It lost credibility when Brasseur de Bourbourg's translation of the Maya script turned out to be wrong.

A more famous name made a brief appearance. Heinrich Schliemann, discoverer and excavator of the sites of Troy and Mycenae, wondered towards the end of his life about ancient Atlantic voyaging and – perhaps – Atlantis. A grandson, Paul Schliemann, professed to have inherited proofs of it, 'the Source of all Civilization'. The great archaeologist had left him unpublished papers about discoveries at Troy, and some artefacts including a bronze vessel inscribed 'From the King Cronos of Atlantis'. Paul padded out his assertions with matter from Donnelly and le Plongeon, but never produced anything to substantiate them.

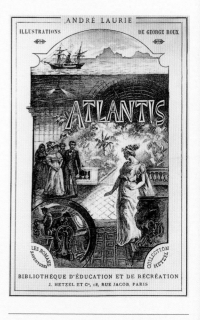

The discovery of Atlantis has always been an ambition, whether it remains under the sea, as in André Laurie's fantasy novel *Atlantis*, 1895 (cover illustration above by George Roux), or is now on land, as in Heinrich Schliemann's *Ilios: City and Country of the Trojans*, 1880 (*opposite*). Schliemann's excavations of Troy might suggest the city as an origin of the Atlantis story.

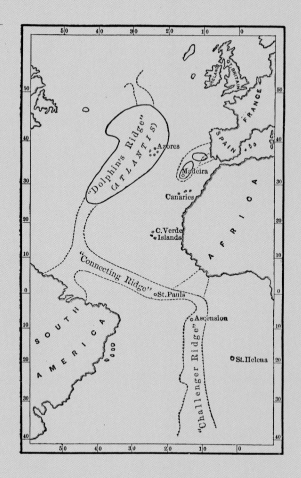

The truth is that a wholly literal reading of Plato cannot be sustained, quite apart from the divine amour at the beginning of the story. Even in 1882 well-informed readers could see that Donnelly had to fudge his chronology. No Athenian republic could have existed in 9500-plus BC. Nor could a civilization have existed using bronze and other metals, carrying out major engineering works, and maintaining warships and horse-drawn chariots. It is no use arguing that the Atlanteans had these things before anyone else, and that they vanished under the sea beyond archaeologists' reach. No evidence has been found in the reputed Atlantean colonies, which did not vanish. The Mid-Atlantic Ridge is solid enough, but apart from the island peaks there is no sign that any part of it has been above water for many millions of years. Neither does geology favour the notion of a large land-mass sinking overnight, in the Atlantic Ocean or anywhere else. So far as is known, major changes in the terrestrial surface do not happen like that.

Supporters of Donnelly have urged that the civilizations of Egypt and Central America appear suddenly, with only scant traces of prior evolution. The inference is that they were both ready-made transplants from a parent civilization that evolved previously in the space between. But neither Egypt nor Central America began as long ago as the 10th millennium BC, nor did they begin at the same time or anywhere near it, nor are they enough alike to imply colonists from a mother country.

## The civilizations of Egypt and Central America appear suddenly, with only scant traces of prior evolution. The inference is that they were both ready-made transplants from a parent civilization ...

When Atlantis did win approval from a scholar of standing, his idea of it was not Plato's, and it was not Donnelly's either, though his approach was akin. This was Lewis Spence, a Scottish anthropologist, who published *The Problem of Atlantis* in 1924 and followed it up with further books. He thought Plato's story was roughly right as to date, but was a literary version of a vague, scattered folk-tradition. In Spence's opinion there were two large Atlantic islands, Atlantis and Antillia, the latter surviving fragmentarily in the West Indies. He rejected Plato's advanced, metal-using society, but observed fairly that a Stone Age society need not have been merely brutish. His basic conception was a 'culture-complex', which he detected both in western Europe and in eastern America. Tell-tale common factors included witchcraft, distinctive burial practices, and head-flattening. 'Occult sciences' flourished. In Europe, Spence's Atlanteans were the Cro-Magnon and Aurignacian people in France and Spain, who painted so vividly on the walls of caves.

Spence made few converts of academic repute. The geological obstacle loomed too large. But his books and Donnelly's, despite their divergence, supplied the main inspiration for a science of Atlantology. One of its more responsible exponents was Egerton Sykes. In English-speaking countries its progress was tranquil, but a French Société d'Études Atlantéennes, founded in 1926, split so acrimoniously that one faction disrupted a meeting of the other with tear-gas bombs.

# CONCEDING the difficulty of finding Atlantis where Plato says, many have theorized that it was somewhere else, was maybe a place known to history, and that traditions of it were garbled and inflated before they drifted down to him.

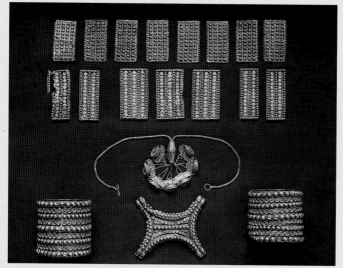

Part of the gold treasure of Tartessus, known as 'El Carambolo', found near Seville and dating from c. 600–550 BC. The city-state of Tartessus has been proposed as the site for the 'real' Atlantis.

➤ The Lady of Elche, sometimes interpreted as an Atlantean priestess. Greco-Iberian bust from Alicante, Spain, c. 400–350 BC.

One candidate is Tartessus, a wealthy city-state said to have existed at the mouth of the Guadalquivir near Cadiz, and to have been the biblical Tarshish. Little is on record about it, and it drops out of history towards 500 BC, a date which raises the objection that it would still have been flourishing when Solon was in Egypt. French and German researchers, noting the Greek allusion to people called Atlantes in Africa, have tried to reconstruct Atlantis around them. On this showing it was centred upon a city in the Sahara which succumbed to sand rather than water. Much was made of a grave in the Ahaggar highlands housing the remains of a rich woman: an Atlantean princess? Modifications of the African theory, one of them offered by Robert Graves, have placed Atlantis in Tunis or Nigeria. Others, however, have found it under the North Sea, in the British Isles, in the megalithic region of ancient Europe, in Crete, in Ceylon, in Cambodia ... and that is nothing like a complete list. The criticism that such guesses cancel each other seems hard to rebut.

One theory, among the oddest of all, remains intriguing not because it locates Atlantis but because it links up with authentic traditions of an abode of Ancient Wisdom. Madame Blavatsky just missed a discovery. She cites Jean Sylvain Bailly, an 18th-century French astronomer, but overlooks a study he made of some astronomical tables discovered in India by missionaries. Bailly found recurrent errors in them. Errors, that is, from the viewpoint of an observer in India. He judged that the tables would be correct from the viewpoint of an observer in the region then known as Tartary, 49 degrees north of the equator. So they must have been compiled there, and taken to India with no adjustment for the different latitude.

> They attained an unprecedented level of culture and, among other feats, compiled the astronomical tables. Wars and migrations carried their descendants still farther …

← Olof Rudbeck reveals the truth of Atlantis to his predecessors in the engraved frontispiece of *Atlantica*, published over the years 1657 to 1698. Rudbeck located Atlantis in Sweden, and was an influence on the French astronomer Jean Sylvain Bailly, who looked farther east to Siberia for the lost city.

Bailly related this to a complicated argument about Atlantis. Plato's island was in the Arctic. It was perhaps Spitzbergen, which, in his opinion, used to be warmer. When the climate grew severe and the population increased, Atlanteans pushed into Siberia between the Ob and Yenisei rivers. The tribes already there withdrew towards Krasnoyarsk and thence to Altaic country around the forty-ninth parallel. Here they attained an unprecedented level of culture and, among other feats, compiled the astronomical tables. Presently the Atlanteans overran that country as well. Wars and migrations carried their descendants still farther south, together with the scientific legacy of the transplanted Ob-Yenisei people.

Bailly's inference about the forty-ninth parallel places his astronomers in the area which the clues to Shambhala indicate. It converges with the Shambhala mythos and incidentally vindicates the Theosophists' interest in it, whatever the value of their attempts (and his) to bring Atlanteans in.

SINCE it leads to so much confusion to read Plato literally or even semi-literally, the only way to shed any light is to ask what he was actually doing and how his mind worked; to take Atlantis, not literally indeed, but seriously.

When he wrote of it Plato was, primarily, creating a myth. That can be said without prejudice to any enquiry into his sources or the factual background. He believed that small well-organized states were better than empires. Empires decayed, city-republics such as Athens had superior moral force, and, though they also could decay, they had a power of regeneration. Not long before Plato's own time Athens had played the leading role in repulsing the aggressive empire of Persia. He evoked an ancient Athens more or less fulfilling his own ideals and thus capable of defeating an even greater empire, the greatest ever. In the making of this political fable, his literary skill – on the face of it – ran away with him, so that he devised a tale far richer, far more circumstantial, than his purpose required.

*The Flood, in Greek mythology as in the Bible and elsewhere, is temporary. The waters ebb and the land reappears, it does not stay submerged as Atlantis does.*

But where did he get the ingredients?

One false clue may be cleared away. The Greeks, like numerous other peoples, had a legend of a great Flood. Plato mentions it in the *Timaeus*. But he does not associate it with the fall of Atlantis, and in fact neither this nor any of the analogous Flood stories can have any relation to it. The Flood, in Greek mythology as in the Bible and elsewhere, is temporary. The waters ebb and the land reappears, it does not stay submerged as Atlantis does.

➤ An allegory of the religions and traditions after the Flood: in Donnelly's terms, legacies of Atlantis, conserving portions of its wisdom in altered forms. Watercolour by Joseph M. Gandy (1771–1843).

Human details are more significant. Atlantis is not a total fantasy-land, it has features suggesting Bronze Age society in the orbit of Bronze Age Greece, the world that engendered Greek heroic mythology, the world of Hercules and the Argonauts and the chariot-riding warriors who clashed at Troy. When Homer describes the visit of Odysseus (otherwise Ulysses) to the Phaeacians, on the island of Scherie, he speaks of a palace shining with gold, silver and copper, and other items of Atlantean type. Minoan Crete, where Theseus fought the Minotaur – Crete with its splendid buildings, warm baths, and beautiful art – also has apt qualities. In its last phase Crete even possessed an empire, though a small-scale one, comprising islands in the Aegean and perhaps part of the mainland. Egyptians had some knowledge of the Cretan domain, calling it Keftiu. The priest who talked with Solon might have given him some hazy account of Keftiu and its collapse, which occurred in the 15th century BC, for reasons still debated.

16th-century BC fresco of a town and harbour from the island of Thera or Santorini, the outpost of Minoan Crete that was devastated by an eruption around the 15th century BC.

If we allow that the priest could have muddled his chronology, or that Solon could have misunderstood him, we might guess that the awkward 'nine thousand years' is a mistake for 'nine hundred'. In that case, counting back from Solon, we would be in the period of Crete's sunset glory. About that time a Minoan outpost, the island of Thera or Santorini 70 miles north, was devastated and partly destroyed by a terrific eruption, which affected Crete itself and other areas in the east Mediterranean. Some account of the Minoan empire, its downfall, and the volcanic disaster that may have played a part could have supplied hints for Plato's story.

But to explain away Atlantis as merely Crete, or rather a wildly inflated Crete, is to rationalize and trivialize, and do less than justice to Plato's genius. That limited domain would not have been adequate to his purpose. It had never produced, and could never have produced, the edifying contrast and crisis he needed: a massive assault by a huge alien empire, thwarted by the moral fibre of Athens. He wanted such an empire, with freedom to fictionalize. Having resolved to centre it on a realm such as Greek images of antiquity (Cretan and otherwise) could suggest – a realm wrecked as a divine judgment by a convulsion of nature – he was able to give that realm the size he required by locating it in the spacious, uncharted west.

He found another hint in the shoals and shallows that were reputed to hinder Atlantic navigation. They could be the barely submerged remains of his imperial island, now sunk beneath the waters but only just. Actually they were products of foreign propaganda. The Carthaginians had been venturing into the outer sea for years, and they tried to deter trade competitors by spreading reports of fog and darkness and obstacles. Most of what they said was exaggeration. Many Greeks accepted it nevertheless, and their belief in an obstructed sea allowed Plato to explain the obstruction as due to an Atlantis below the surface.

*All around the land-mass was the outer sea, or Ocean, regarded as an immense river flowing counter-clockwise. We might suppose that they had no idea of anything lying farther out still, but in fact they had.*

There was more to his conception than that. It was not fantasized out of nothing, it fitted into a framework of ideas already established. Greeks had notions of their own about the Atlantic which antedated the shoal delusion, and some were very ancient indeed. In their traditional image of the world, the inhabited land-mass was a disc surrounded by water. The Mediterranean was the inner sea. All around the land-mass was the outer sea, or Ocean, regarded as an immense river flowing counter-clockwise. We might suppose that they had no idea of anything lying farther out still, but in fact they had. As far back as their beliefs can be traced, they pictured trans-Oceanic land of some sort, beyond the western horizon.

Homer's tale of Odysseus takes him across to a place where he consults the shades of the dead. Directed by the enchantress Circe, on an island apparently in the Adriatic, he sails south and then west, out through the Straits of Gibraltar, and across the River of Ocean to the 'frontiers of the world' where the Cimmerians live in mist and gloom. After encountering the shades, he re-embarks, and Ocean's current, circling counter-clockwise, carries him back to the point of entry to the Mediterranean. Whether or not the Cimmerians are in the British Isles, Odysseus crosses Ocean transversely north to reach them. Its stream separates their country from continental Europe.

→ *The Titan's Goblet*, 1833, by Thomas Cole. The huge cup – so large that it contains boats and buildings – is usually interpreted as a kind of relic. The artist may have intended the goblet as a symbol of a mighty, forgotten past, an enigmatic reminder of other civilizations before our own.

Homer also mentions a happier region across the Ocean, as we have seen – the idyllic plain of Elysium, home of heroes beloved of the gods and exempt from death. This is the sunset paradise which, in other Greek writings, sometimes takes the form of the Isles of the Blest or Fortunate Isles. The west and north-west were associated with Cronus, chief of the Titans whom Zeus banished. Cronus's place of exile lay in that quarter, and he was reputed to rule a consolation kingdom across the Ocean, perhaps in the paradisal country itself. Atlas, who gave his name to Atlantis, was originally one of these banished Titans. Other myths located the Gorgons and the Garden of the Hesperides in western islands.

Geographers in later years identified the islands with real ones, such as Madeira and the Canaries. Probably these were not known when the myths took shape, and the identifications were afterthoughts. What matters is that 'land to the west' was an established motif when Plato wrote. His evocation of Atlantis was a creative leap, but a leap in conformity with a scattering of respected traditions, not a fancy out of nowhere.

He may have drawn on other ideas about the west. Travellers' tales of megalithic monuments, in lands such as Britain bordering the Atlantic, could have conjured up a vanished people with capabilities beyond those of the current inhabitants. To judge from traces of trade, Britain may have been dimly known for a while and then lost sight of, so that it might have been supposed to have disappeared. Moreover, it could supply an actual mini-Atlantis, Mount's Bay in Cornwall, forested and peopled till about 1500 BC but afterwards flooded. Its inundation, and the later subsidence of land connecting the Isles of Scilly, shaped the Cornish legend of lost Lethowstow, which became the Lyonesse of romance.

*Travellers' tales of megalithic monuments, in lands such as Britain bordering the Atlantic, could have conjured up a vanished people with capabilities beyond those of the current inhabitants.*

That is as far as it is safe to go. Yet a further question can be asked. When Plato planted his conception in the far west, was he merely synthesizing one more island, albeit a big one, among the islands already fancied there? Or was he grounding it (so to speak) as a purported description of a place known to exist, or to have existed? That was the view taken in the Age of Discovery when Atlantis was 'found' in America. It raises the issue of geographical knowledge. An intriguing datum here is Plato's non-functional throwaway line about other islands beyond Atlantis, and an 'opposite continent'.

His words are not as indicative of America as they look. The continent is not merely across the Ocean, it goes all the way round, enclosing it with an outer rim and extending indefinitely beyond. But it has a feature of special interest. It makes other literary appearances in classical times. One of them has been thought to imply that it is an extrapolation from a real American contact.

From that point of view, its first appearance is not at
all encouraging. Theopompus, a younger contemporary of
Plato, quotes a very far-fetched account of the trans-Oceanic
continent. It has colossal animals; it has humans twice the size
of ourselves, who once invaded our world ten million strong,
but were so little impressed that they went back again; it has
fruits that afflict those who eat them with perpetual grief,
and fruits that make their eaters happy but also make them
grow younger and younger till they vanish. ... Appropriately,
Theopompus puts these and other fables in the mouth of
Silenus, a drunken companion of the wine-god Dionysus. They
prompted Graves's theory that the dramatist Thespis retorted
to abuse from Solon by making fun of his Atlantis talk. He
might have done this in a type of comedy known as a satyr-play.
Satyr-plays had Silenus in them as a stock comic character,
and Thespis could have brought him in spinning this yarn. At
least the notion of the far continent is here, however derived,
however preposterously handled.

St Michael's Mount, Cornwall,
formerly a hill surrounded by a forest
that is now under the sea – a real
small-scale Atlantis.

Plutarch, in the 1st century AD, is more interesting. He wrote philosophic dialogues like Plato. In one of them he discusses the markings on the moon, the people who may live there, and other topics including Atlantic crossings. He involves the latter in complications about his sources quite in the style of Plato himself. However, it is possible to piece together an account of voyagers sailing west from Britain to a land with adjacent islands where the summer night is less than an hour long. After some months they go on across a sea 500 or 600 miles wide, impeded by ice and debris, to 'the great continent by which the Ocean is fringed', and coast around to a bay with its mouth in about the same latitude as the north end of the Caspian Sea (Plutarch says its outlet, but, like many Greeks, he does not realize that the Caspian is land-locked; its north end was thought to open into the Ocean).

Mythical animals populate *Buenos Aires, America* (detail of *The Four Parts of the World*) by Jan van Kessel, 1666. Though a large part of America had been colonized by the time this artist worked, there was still scope for daydreaming about the land beyond the western ocean.

All this, with further details, is the setting for a myth about Cronus, the westward-banished Titan, lying asleep in an island on the far side. But the geography fits the facts rather well. It could apply to the northern trans-Atlantic route, the Viking route. The voyagers go from the north end of Britain to southern Greenland, where the summer night is very short, then across the Davis Strait to Labrador and around to the Gulf of St Lawrence. The forty-seventh parallel traverses not only the Gulf's main outlet between Newfoundland and Cape Breton Island, but also the north end of the Caspian Sea.

To revert to Plato, his own implied map can be reconstructed in outline. Unlike myth-makers before him, he knew the Earth to be spherical. He pictured our inhabited land-mass as in the midst of an Ocean that was really a gigantic lake. To accommodate Atlantis and the islands beyond, he gave this a western bulge, the Atlantic. Beyond again was the coast that swept around to enclose the Ocean on every side. The rest of Earth's surface was presumably land, the 'boundless continent'.

Plato pictured our inhabited land-mass as in the midst of an Ocean that was really a gigantic lake. ... The rest of Earth's surface was presumably land, the 'boundless continent'.

Was that continent purely conceptual, or did any Greeks know of the New World and jump to the conclusion that it went all the way round? Plutarch may imply as much. Plato owes no evident debt to the particular Greek knowledge he may imply, knowledge of the northern route, and Greenland and Canada. Yet if the possibility of knowledge is admitted at all, it is worthwhile to glance, finally, at one of the few classical authors who did believe in Atlantis.

This is Proclus, a philosopher of the Neo-Platonic school, who wrote a commentary on the *Timaeus* between 432 and 440 AD. He is not normally literal-minded, but where Atlantis is concerned, he becomes so.

That such and so great an island once existed, is evident from what is said by certain historians respecting what pertains to the external sea [i.e., the sea outside the Mediterranean]. For according to them, there were seven islands in that sea, in their times, sacred to Proserpine, and also three others of an immense extent, one of which was sacred to Pluto, another to Ammon, and the middle (or second) of these to Neptune, the magnitude of which was a thousand stadia. They also add that the inhabitants of it preserved the remembrance from their ancestors, of the Atlantic island which existed there, and was truly prodigiously great; which for many periods had dominion over all the islands in the Atlantic sea, and was likewise sacred to Neptune. These things Marcellus writes in his Ethiopic history.

*Proclus is giving a glimpse of earlier matter, possibly early enough to have been known to Plato; and apart from the religious touches, he would make tolerable sense if we could allow that his islands are the Antilles, the main chain of the West Indies.*

Proclus also cites the earlier commentator Crantor. He claims that there were columns in Egypt with the story of Atlantis displayed on them, and that other Neo-Platonists have shared his belief. The noteworthy thing, however, is this transcript or paraphrase from Marcellus. Marcellus lived in the 1st century BC and his work is lost, so we have no way of directly checking. Yet Proclus is giving a glimpse of earlier matter, possibly early enough to have been known to Plato; and apart from the religious touches, he would make tolerable sense if we could allow that his islands are the Antilles, the main chain of the West Indies.

---

◄— Fragment of an anonymous world map, c. 1450. North is at the bottom. It shows part of Europe, the Mediterranean, and a very approximate Africa. The ocean has fabulous islands in it; one may be the home of the Hesperides and another a place of immortality.

First, the seven islands: the principal Lesser Antilles can be fairly counted as seven, namely Guadeloupe, Dominica, Martinique, St Lucia, Barbados, St Vincent, Grenada. Then, the three large ones: the greater members of the chain (Jamaica lies outside it) are just three, Cuba, Hispaniola and Puerto Rico. 'Immense' may sound extreme, but all three are big by Proclus's Mediterranean standards, and he shows what he is prepared to call 'immense' when he gives the breadth of the middle one as a thousand stadia, a little over 100 miles – which is close enough to the actual breadth of Hispaniola. Furthermore, the native Caribs and the tribes of Hispaniola itself did have a sort of Atlantis tradition. They said many of the islands had once been connected, as parts of a single mass, but a cataclysm ages ago had submerged the connections and left only the fragments they lived upon.

*The native Caribs and the tribes of Hispaniola itself did have a sort of Atlantis tradition. They said many of the islands had once been connected ... but a cataclysm ages ago had submerged the connections ...*

There is a bare chance that Proclus is on the right track. Thanks to unrecorded explorers, some report of these islands, and the islanders, and their tale of ancient disaster, may have got back to Greece. Whatever the uniting land was actually called, Plato may have seized on it as the lost Atlantis he wanted, and 'described' it in terms suggested by Homeric legend and traditions of Crete, the only antiquity he felt at ease with. The land would coincide partly with Lewis Spence's Antillia. Spence did not derive this name from the Antilles. On the contrary, 'Antilles' is derived from 'Antillia', which was the name given to an island that pre-Columbian geographers, such as Toscanelli, speculated about; Spence adopted it from them. No one knows how they hit on it to begin with, but it has been explained as a corruption of 'Atlantis' itself. At any rate, the nearest we can get to a meaningful 'real Atlantis' is seemingly in and around the West Indies – which have historically been subject to eruptions and earthquakes. The visionary Edgar Cayce, with his revelation about the Bahamas, may not have been too wide of the mark.

➤ Thomas More's vision of Atlantis as an island. Woodcut by Ambrosius Holbein from a 1518 edition of *Utopia*.

In the upshot Plato overreached himself. His doomed Atlanteans outshone his virtuous Athenians. To quote James Bramwell, author of *Lost Atlantis*:

> The prehistoric Greeks, whose civilization is intended to be the ideal of simple goodness and classic restraint, seem frankly dull, whereas the lavish and luxurious Atlantean civilization ... transcends all questions of 'taste' by its strong appeal to the imagination and the sense. ... The fate of the Greeks is not interesting; Atlantis and its citizens are the 'heroes' of the drama and the reader's sympathies are with them from the beginning. ... There is tragic irony in the description of the material splendour and vast scale of the city, its wealth of colour and movement, its elaborate political organization. ... When it is overwhelmed by the sea, the tragedy lies in the uniqueness of the marvel that is lost to the world. ... One feels that Plato was so carried away from his original intention by the poetry of the theme, that the fable got beyond his control.

By his feat of creative synthesis he supplied the material for a myth quite different from his own, and this, the *modern* myth of Atlantis, emerged after many centuries.

◄— A wave sweeping into a devastated town. The scene was inspired by legends of St Januarius, patron of Naples, who is associated with preserving the city from such disasters as eruptions of Vesuvius. Early 17th-century painting by Monsù Desiderio.

—► *The Course of Empire: Destruction*, 1836, by Thomas Cole, suggests a relentless pattern of ruin-following-glory. The gigantic statue of a warrior holding up a useless shield symbolizes a past power ineffectual against advancing doom. The destruction is due to natural forces, not human agency.

Just so. By his feat of creative synthesis he supplied the material for a myth quite different from his own, and this, the *modern* myth of Atlantis, emerged after many centuries. The architect of transition was Ignatius Donnelly. Because of him, innumerable people became aware of Atlantis, and believed it to have been real as he portrayed it; and he persuaded them with arguments giving it an importance and marvellousness transcending even Plato's conception. Madame Blavatsky and the other occultists added their contribution, but it largely presupposed Donnelly, and would have made only a limited impression apart from him.

# POWERFUL as occultism became in promotion,

Atlantis could attract novelists and dramatists without it, or with only a moderate amount. In this respect as in others Jules Verne had already been, though briefly, a trail-blazer; he may have played a part in launching Donnelly himself on his enterprise.

Verne's *Twenty Thousand Leagues Under the Sea* (1870) is pioneering science-fiction. The narrator is a French naturalist, Professor Aronnax. With two companions he is captured by Captain Nemo ('Nobody'), the inventor and master of a wonderful submarine, the *Nautilus*. The novel tells of mysterious wanderings through the oceans, which give Aronnax enviable opportunities for studying marine life. Every so often Nemo lends his guests diving suits and takes them out for walks on the sea-bed. On one of these he shows Aronnax a ruined city. Talk being impossible in the diving suits, he identifies the ruins by writing ATLANTIS. Aronnax, aware of the literary background, is excited to learn that the story has a basis. This is only an incident and Verne does not follow it up. They return to the *Nautilus* and the voyage continues.

Among works of fiction which are Atlantis-centred, C. J. Cutcliffe Hyne's *The Lost Continent* (1899) is outstanding. It is slightly reminiscent of the romances of Rider Haggard, such as *She* (1887). A prologue recounts the discovery of a manuscript in a cave in the Canary Islands. Written on durable sheets in characters resembling Egyptian, it gives its author's name as Deucalion. The discoverers recall that a Deucalion was the Greek version of Noah. Divinely warned of the imminent Flood, he built a boat and survived with his wife.

Portrait of Jules Verne, 1856.

→ An 1896 illustration of Jules Verne's *Twenty Thousand Leagues Under the Sea* by Alphonse de Neuville. Captain Nemo and the tale's narrator, Professor Aronnax, search for a ruined city under the sea.

The real Deucalion turns out to have been an Atlantean officer of state, and the novel, presented as a translation of his manuscript, takes the form of a first-person memoir. Atlantis is a civilized imperial power, without extreme occult features, though there are touches of magic and allusions to awesome Mysteries. Back in the capital after a colonial governorship, Deucalion is shocked at the decline which has set in under a brilliant but tyrannical empress. She wants to marry him to consolidate her position, and he consents from patriotic motives, hoping to influence her, though he loves another woman. Their joint reign never materializes. She changes her mind and he finds himself endangered. After several years in hiding he returns again to the capital at the height of a conflict between the empress, who has proclaimed herself divine, and the priests of the old religion. Terrible secret forces are unleashed and Atlantis sinks. Deucalion and his true love survive in an ark prepared by the priests for such an eventuality. It contains writings setting forth the Mysteries. He finds them so frightening that he erases the text, and Atlantis's Ancient Wisdom is lost. However, the couple reach land, and the story ends by linking up with its Greek pseudo-derivative.

*The House of the Atlantides*, 1919, a sketch by German Expressionist artist Hermann Finsterlin. He experimented with plastic architectural forms, reflecting mystical and utopian speculations, and defying customary concepts of function and meaning.

➤ Illustration from the 1870 French edition of *Twenty Thousand Leagues Under the Sea*. Captain Nemo and Professor Aronnax view a ruined underwater city with a submarine volcano erupting close by.

L. Sprague de Camp, biographer of the fantasy writer H. P. Lovecraft, and authority on the Atlantis story, contributed to the fiction in *Tritonian Ring*. There is a trilogy by Jane Gaskell. Pierre Benoit's *L'Atlantide* exploits the African theory and locates Atlantis in what is now the Sahara. Atlantean survival into modern times has commended itself to other novelists besides Conan Doyle. Abraham Merritt, in *The Face in the Abyss,* imagines a colony concealed in the Andes. Victor Rousseau takes up the notion of Atlanteans living inside the Earth. Dennis Wheatley diverges from horror and satanism in *They Found Atlantis.* Near the beginning of this novel, the scientist who has planned the search presents his case to a potential backer; Wheatley handles it knowledgeably, though he invents extra evidence that would, in real life, make a crucial difference. The Atlantis which is 'found' is a tiny, paradisal remnant in a hidden space below the Azores. Its inhabitants – heirs of an unparalleled civilization – are very wise, very good, and, by their own choice, very few. Their community has remained in being through ancestral paranormal powers. They visit the upper world in spirit but make no attempt to reach it.

*The Atlantis which is 'found' is a tiny, paradisal remnant in a hidden space below the Azores. Its inhabitants – heirs of an unparalleled civilization – are very wise, very good, and, by their own choice, very few.*

Lemuria or Mu, lacking similar credentials, has had little fictional attention apart from forays in magazines such as *Amazing Stories.* A tongue-in-cheek novel is *The Monster of Mu,* by Owen Rutter. Near Easter Island some treasure-hunters discover another island which is a remnant of Mu. Its chief inhabitants are immortal Muvian priests, ruling over a smaller brown-skinned populace. The priests have a taboo on women. Refusing to make an exception for a female member of the party, they try to sacrifice her to a plesiosaur. Nature effects a rescue. The island sinks, and one of the treasure-hunters escapes with the intended victim.

A few Atlantis films have been made, including a version of Benoit's Sahara novel, but none with a high place in cinematic history. More important is an epic, *L'Atlantida,* by the Catalan poet Jacinto Verdaguer (1845–1902). This was the basis of a semi-operatic work by Manuel de Falla (1876–1946), a leading figure in Spanish music, composer of the ballet *The Three-Cornered Hat.* His *Atlantida,* for chorus, soloists and orchestra, was incomplete at his death. Finished by a pupil, it was performed in 1961.

An ambitious curiosity is a 'fantasy with music' called *Atalanta*, composed around 1950 by Sir Gerald Hargreaves, a judge. The libretto and portions of the score were published in book form. *Atalanta* has never been staged – it is too long, the casting requirements are excessive, and the cost of Sir Gerald's sets would be prohibitive – yet it repays a passing look. The Hargreaves Atlantis is more or less the Atlantis of Plato, but the date is moved so as to make Homeric Troy one of its colonies. Its unsuccessful attack on the Greeks is provoked by their successful attack on Troy. The characters include Agamemnon, Menelaus, Helen, and other old friends. Despite the gravity of the main events, Sir Gerald maintains a light-hearted tone. Even Atlantis's sinking, reported briefly, becomes a sort of fairy-tale doom that prompts no thoughts of real death or destruction. The speeches and lyrics are sometimes reminiscent of W. S. Gilbert, and the music, correspondingly, is sometimes reminiscent of his theatrical partner and composer Arthur Sullivan.

# WHY

this fascination, most of it in the last hundred-odd years, with a myth invented long ago by a Greek philosopher? Why the persistent attempts to find literal truth in it when most of Plato's fellow Greeks did not?

For many of those involved, the allure is simply that of a riddle or romance. However, others believe it goes deeper, and without their enthusiasm it is doubtful whether the simpler allure would have lasted. Atlantis is not merely a territory swallowed up by the sea, like, say, the land formerly joining England to France. It is not merely a theme for geographic debate, or volcanic or seismic speculation. Its spell is inherent, compelling, and strong enough to lend credibility to theories that are often incredible.

*Atlantis is not merely a territory swallowed up by the sea. ... It is not merely a theme for geographic debate ... Its spell is inherent, compelling, and strong enough to lend credibility to theories that are often incredible.*

Once again, though, the modern myth is not Plato's. Hargreaves, the amateur of light opera, is exceptional in sticking to this. Apart from him, the enthusiasts keep the spotlight on Atlantis itself, and Plato's noble Athenians, who were the occasion for the whole story, fade out. While Atlantis's decline and fall are admitted, they are seldom linked with the crime of aggression or the inferiority of empires to republics. For this change, turning Plato's creation into something else, he has only himself to thank. Even though, in another dialogue, he says he would exclude poets from his ideal state, his description of the lost land is a flight of poetic imagination, and it ranges so far beyond his requirements as to excuse a feeling that there is more here than meets the eye, that there must be something in it.

➤ The model for *Atlantis*, 1987, by Carl Laubin, was the architect Léon Krier's designs for a utopian mini-city avoiding rectangularity and grid-patterning.

Rethought by Donnelly and the rest as the fountain-head of civilization, Atlantis combines and opens up certain themes, recurrent and haunting themes that take a variety of forms. It stands for the Golden Age and it stands for Ancient Wisdom, which are linked, with Ancient Wisdom frequently more conspicuous. Mythology in general tends to place these things in a tragic scenario. The Golden Age ended long ago; Ancient Wisdom is partially eclipsed and recoverable only piecemeal, never in its pristine fullness. Atlantis, with its glory and enlightenment and Higher Mysteries, its decay through perverted powers or loss of vision, and its apocalyptic collapse, is the grandest of imagined contexts for the archetypal drama.

On all this, the stance and role of Theosophy are clear. But some authors are more akin to Blake. A book by a well-known New Age exponent, John Michell, is entitled *The View Over Atlantis* (1969). Strangely, yet significantly, Atlantis hardly appears in it. Atlantis has come to symbolize a medley of Ancient Wisdom motifs – Druid lore, the inner meaning of megaliths and the Great Pyramid, sacred geometry, and much else. These secrets, which we are the worse for losing, can be unriddled and recaptured.

> Written across the face of the country in letters of earth and stone the cosmic knowledge of the ancient world is now within reach. It appears that in recent ages the human race has lost touch with some hidden source of power, some ultimate proof of cosmic order which inspired the monumental achievements of antiquity and produced the serene confidence of prehistoric life.

Atlantis is brought in explicitly only here and there, on the vague Donnelly-derivative ground that 'the former existence of a universal civilization is seen to be inevitable'. All the topics discussed, taken together, imply that it *must have* been real. The inference may be sound in a very general way. It may be that a senior culture, undefined at present, did spread its influence through historic ancient civilizations. However, that is no good reason to jump to an Atlantean conclusion. Atlantis, here, is simply a time-honoured and exciting place to locate it.

← *Morning. Fantasy. Enchanted City*, 1904, a pastel drawing by Mikalojus Čiurlionis, whose oblique, allusive imagery embodied aspirations and archetypes, sometimes echoing Atlantean themes.

John Michell favours the belief which recurs in Atlantean imaginings as it occurs elsewhere, that the lost glory is not truly lost, or, at any rate, not altogether. For him it is a corpus of Ancient Wisdom that can be recovered by deciphering messages encoded in the works of antiquity. In much the same spirit Colin Amery looks to the discovery of the Hall of Records in Egypt, and Randall-Stevens predicts that Atlantis will resurface.

To go back to Madame Blavatsky, her logic resembled John Michell's. Ancient Wisdom, she declared, was veiled in myths and symbols which only initiates understood, and was preserved by Masters and other illuminated beings. Although Atlantis was not their home, it manifested their powers. As remarked before, though she acknowledged the Asian wisdom-centre Shambhala and connected it with Atlantis, she missed the notable theory of Jean Sylvain Bailly, who related his own far-northern Atlantis, and his astronomers in Tartary, to a broader scheme of the origins of civilization. For him the 'senior culture' did exist, and in more or less Altaic country in Central Asia, roughly where lamaistic tradition locates Shambhala ... which he knew nothing of. As it happens, there is now a case for suspecting a real cultural seed-bed in that part of the world, with a significant effect on real history, its former importance echoed in the Shambhala mythos. With Bailly at least, Atlantean speculation may have pointed towards an actual quasi-Atlantis, less spectacular than the one in the ocean, but by no means negligible.*

However it may be with the Shambhalic and Antillian possibilities, the Atlantis of modern imagination reflects a desire to draw threads together, to unravel mysteries, to fill what is felt to be a historical gap with a key to the cipher – with a great wonderful Something Else that *should* have existed, and corresponds to perennial yearnings. And who knows? Perhaps the instinct is sound, perhaps there actually was a Something Else that will come to light. Plato planted a seed he never meant to plant. He set people thinking on lines that may eventually prove to be fruitful.

→ Explorers discovering the lost city of Shambhala. Drawing from Alan Grant and Arthur Ranson's *Shamballa*, 1991.

* I have explored this field in two books: *The Ancient Wisdom* (1977) and *Dawn Behind the Dawn* (1992).

# PLATO'S PARADOX

There is only one direct witness to Atlantis's existence, and he is puzzling, even contradictory.

The witness is the Greek philosopher Plato. As a young man he knew Socrates. After the latter's death he presided over a circle in Athens, and wrote imaginary conversations or 'dialogues' portraying Socrates talking with friends. Some of these may be true to life; in others, Plato uses the characters as mouthpieces for teachings and stories of his own.

Two of the dialogues are entitled *Timaeus* and *Critias* after the principal speakers in them. Passages in both tell of an island-continent in the western ocean. Formerly a domain of the sea-god Poseidon, it was named Atlantis after Atlas the Titan, said to have been Poseidon's son. It had a magnificent capital. Its people made use of gold, silver, bronze and tin, and also orichalcum, a rather mysterious alloy. Atlantis's kings conquered parts of Europe and Africa and a trans-Atlantic continent. At last the Athenians defeated them. Then, in a cataclysm of flood and earthquake, Atlantis sank bodily beneath the sea.

The first thing to understand is that Plato has created a paradox, Atlantis is a problem which, in a plain straightforward sense, has no solution. That is one reason why it fascinates, and has inspired dozens of interpretations. Plato simultaneously builds up and tears down, making it convincing or at least plausible, yet also – apparently – impossible. He supports the story with masses of circumstantial detail and a precise account of its transmission via Critias's family from the lawgiver Solon, who heard it from an Egyptian priest better informed about Greek history than the Greeks themselves. The impression is certainly that Plato did not invent it. But the war and Atlantis's collapse are dated more than nine thousand years before his time, when the civilization he describes could not possibly have existed. Nor could his victorious Athens.

Atlas holds the heavens on his shoulders.
Laconian cup, c. 560.

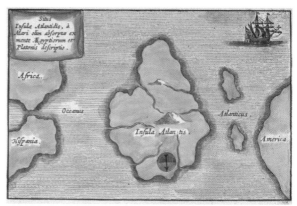

An imaginary map of Atlantis. Engraving from Athanasius Kircher's
*Mundus subterraneus*, 1678.

Head of Poseidon, c. 460 BC.

Atlantis's capital city, based on Plato's description. Illustration after Walter Heiland from Albert Herrmann's *Unsere Ahnen und Atlanten*, 1934.

Atlantis as imagined by Paul Schliemann. He claimed to have inherited secret proofs from his grandfather, the discoverer of the site of Troy.

Herm of Plato (427–347 BC) thought to be an authentic likeness.

# THE MAKING OF A MYTH

Whatever its basis, the Atlantis story is presented as a moral fable. It has a background in a war fought some decades before Plato's birth, when Athens took the lead in repulsing a Persian attack on Greece. Though far from fulfilling his political ideals, Athens had at least proved a city-state's superiority to an empire. That was a lesson which Plato wanted to improve on. He pictured an ancient Athens that did resemble his own ideal republic, and foiled the aggression of an empire even greater than Persia.

Atlantis as he evoked it owed some of its features to Minoan Crete, ancient scene of the legends of the Minotaur and Labyrinth: maritime rule, opulent palaces, warm baths, a bull-cult. But it is hard to see these as more than descriptive trappings for a huge alien power which he knew had never existed in the Mediterranean. It belonged outside. Greeks already took a mythified view of the outer Ocean, imagining wonderful lands across it, the Isles of the Blest or the Garden of the Hesperides. Whether or not Plato also picked up an Egyptian tradition (factual or otherwise) of 'land to the west', he had space and precedent in the Atlantic. On an island larger than those previously imagined, he built up the image of an imperial federation, with a navy, and dominion over lesser islands, and portions of the continents both eastward and westward – the latter possibly reflecting a vague awareness of the New World.

That was the Atlantis of his myth. Since it was no longer there, at any rate within the range of Greek seamanship, he had to explain why not. He attributed its absence to a convulsion of nature. Here he may have taken a further hint from traditions of the Minoan world. The Aegean island of Thera (Santorini) was smashed by a tremendous eruption in the 15th century BC, during the last decades of Crete's importance.

Minoan Crete influenced the description of Atlantis. Reconstruction of 'The Queen's Megaron' from Arthur Evans's *Palace of Minos at Knossos*, 1923–36.

Oceanus, the outer Ocean personified. Mosaic from Hadrimentum (Sousse), AD 150–200.

Ships of the type in which Greeks acquired knowledge of the sea. Cup from Cerveteri signed by Nikosthenes, c. 520 BC.

*The Minotaur*, the monster inside the Cretan Labyrinth, by George Frederick Watts, c. 1877–86.

Greeks fighting Persians. Plato's account of the collapse of the Atlantean empire took a hint from the defeat of Persia. Relief from the Alexander Sarcophagus, late 4th century BC.

Cretan imagery of a ritual bull-dance. The Atlanteans reputedly sacrificed bulls. Seal impression from Achat.

The Hesperides in their garden. Painting by Hans von Marées, 1885.

# DEATH BY WATER

Inundation is a recurrent theme of mythology. The biblical Deluge has many parallels. There is a Greek version which Plato mentions, though he does not associate it with Atlantis.

Very old and influential is the Mesopotamian legend. The fullest account is in the Babylonian epic of Gilgamesh. The hero visits Utnapishtim, who survived the disaster and is now immortal. Utnapishtim tells how he was warned of the gods' intention to wipe out a troublesome humanity. He built an ark, and stayed afloat with his wife and other companions. When the waters subsided the ark came to rest on a mountain-top.

The biblical story is related to this, but has an added moral dimension. God sends the Flood as a judgment on human wickedness, and preserves Noah and his family because they are righteous. Here, likewise, the ark comes to rest on a mountain, Ararat. There is no reason to think Plato knew the Hebrew story, but in *Critias*, though it is unfinished, he is clearly treating Atlantis's destruction as a divine judgment.

In Hindu mythology the god Krishna protects people from a flood by moving a mountain, but the city of Dwaraka, home of his earthly kinsfolk, is swallowed up itself by the ocean. These are local events. Much longer ago, the whole earth was submerged. Again we hear of an ark and a mountain-top. The survivors are the divine lawgiver Manu and the Seven Rishis, Hinduism's masters of Ancient Wisdom.

The collapse of Atlantis, whether invented or in some sense historical, differs from the happenings in these Flood stories by being permanent. The waters remain, the land never re-emerges. Attempts to argue that the Flood stories themselves derive from the sinking of a real Atlantis, and are therefore evidence for it, must be seen as dubious.

*The Flood* by David Humbert de Superville (1770–1849).

The Flood: *Sonata of the Sea* by Mikalojus Čiurlionis, 1908.

The Mesopotamian 'Noah' with his boat. Cylinder seal, early 3rd millennium BC.

The god Krishna moving Mount Govardhan to protect his people from the water. Mughal miniature, c. 1590.

Noah's Ark on the rising biblical floodwaters. Engraving from Athanasius Kircher's *Arca Noë*, 1675.

A Babylonian tablet relating part of the epic of Gilgamesh with the Flood episode, one of many such stories supposedly inspired by the drowning of Atlantis.

# WHEN AND WHERE?

Few of Plato's fellow Greeks took Atlantis literally. Yet his account is so impressive that there have been many attempts to find a factual basis. Some readers have simply believed it. Others, aware of difficulties, have speculated about a tradition that was garbled before it reached him: one that originally referred to another place, another time.

After the opening-up of the New World, several authors concluded that Atlantis was America. The obvious objection was that America was still there. Investigators have pointed to small-scale Atlantises, such as the former wooded tract under Mount's Bay in Cornwall, part of legendary Lyonesse. Could Atlantis have been launched by a more spectacular submergence of the same type, later misplaced and misunderstood?

The Thera eruption has been claimed as a key, not merely to the working of Plato's imagination, but to the origin of the whole story. Thera was an outpost of Minoan Crete, and Atlantis's Cretan touches are admitted. Perhaps Plato's Atlantean empire was simply the Minoan, long since defunct, and exaggerated and set adrift by the passing of nine centuries? A related theory focuses on the war. Solon's Egyptian informant may have recalled an alliance of 'Sea Peoples' who succeeded to Minoan maritime power and threatened Egypt. They included Tyrrhenians and Libyans, both mentioned by Plato. It has even been suggested that it might be Troy and its devastation in the Trojan War, as related in Homer's epics, that gave rise to the legend. The trouble is, however, that there are too many such conjectures, professedly pinning down the 'real Atlantis' not only in the Mediterranean but in widely separated parts of the world.

The American seer Edgar Cayce delivered messages in a trance about the West Indies having been part of Atlantis. His revelations happen to agree fairly well both with hints by Proclus, one of the few Greek authors who believed in it, and with folk memories among the Caribs about a sunken land formerly connecting their islands. If a literal Atlantis is wanted, Cayce's hint seems as good as any.

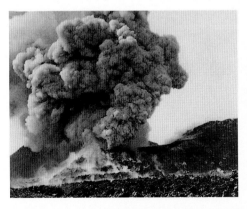

Volcanic action on the island of Thera (Santorini), 1925.

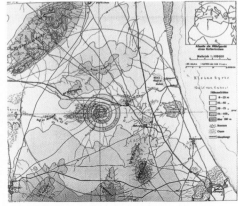

Atlantis in North Africa: another relocation. From Dr A. Petermann's *Mittheilungen aus Justus Perthes' Geographischer Anstalt*, part 73, 1927.

Columbus reaching the West Indies, where the native Caribs had a tradition that their islands were once part of a single land-mass. Woodcut from 1493.

Atlantis by the Red Sea. Detail of a map from Carl Friedrich Baer's *Essai sur les Atlantiques*, 1762.

Egyptians under Rameses III fighting the Sea Peoples in a war which the story of Atlantis's aggression may echo. Relief from Medinet Habu, c. 1190 BC.

# EARTHLY PARADISES

Plato describes his ideal society in the *Republic*, a dialogue to which *Timaeus* and *Critias* are sequels. In them it is ancient Athens and not Atlantis that is made out to have realized his ideal, more or less. With the revival of fiction of this type in the Renaissance, there are the makings of an eventual shift.

Thomas More, inventor in 1516 of the term 'Utopia', places his imaginary commonwealth on an island and not in any known country. Francis Bacon presently restores the Platonic name in *The New Atlantis*, but with a surprising twist. For him, as for some others in this period, Plato's Atlantis is America. His own 'new' one is an island, but an island beyond, with institutions that embody his hopes for the advance of science.

The first hint of Atlantis itself becoming Utopian is in the poetic mythology of William Blake. He speaks of an Atlantic continent uniting the Old and New Worlds, and involves it with the broader themes of Ancient Wisdom and a past Golden Age. Many myths, both old and recent, envision a Golden Age in one way or another. In Christianity it is the paradisal life of Eden, forfeited through the Fall, when Adam and Eve disobeyed God. Blake's complex equivalent of this event includes the vanishing of his Atlantis 'now barr'd out by the Atlantic sea' – a disaster that is functional in his scheme, because it divides the world's peoples.

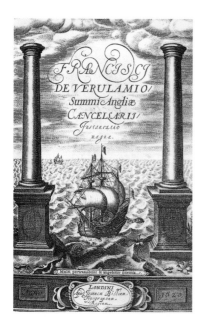

St Brendan searching for the Earthly Paradise on the Atlantic. Engraving from *Nova typis transacta navigatio*, 1621, by Honorio Philopono [Plautius].

Ships sailing westward through the 'Pillars of Hercules' in the Age of Discovery. Engraved title-page to the volume containing Sir Francis Bacon's *New Atlantis*, 1628.

A more sophisticated paradisal concept: *A Vision of Paradise*. Pen and watercolour drawing by Joseph M. Gandy (1771–1843).

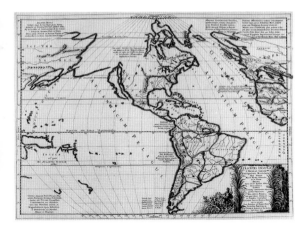

America as the real Atlantis divided into ten kingdoms. Engraved map
from N. and G. Sanson's *Cartes générales*, 1670.

*Paradise* by Herri met de Bles, *c*. 1541–50.

Paradise regained. Illumination by
the Limbourg brothers from the
*Très Riches Heures du Duc de Berry*,
1409–15.

Sir Thomas More's Utopia.
Woodcut by Ambrosius Holbein
from More's *Utopia*, 1518.

Plate 10 of William Blake's *America. A Prophecy*,
1793, containing his lines on the magnificence
of the sunken Atlantic continent.

# THE MYTH RE-MADE

When Plato evoked a model society as existing long ago – his ancient Athens, triumphant over Atlantean aggression, though itself extinguished – his mind was working in conformity with the Golden Age pattern. But he made the aggressors so interesting that he laid the basis for a quite different myth. Modern imagination transfers the long-lost glory to Atlantis itself, giving it an importance that transcends even Plato's flamboyant fancy.

The modern Atlantis myth (properly so called, whatever factual ingredients it may have) was launched in 1882 by an Irish-American politician, Ignatius Donnelly. Broad in his interests, he anticipated H. G. Wells with a novel set in the late 20th century, portraying a plutocracy that collapses, and the birth of an enlightened republic in Africa. His idealism led him to reflect on the past as well as the future.

Soundings in the Atlantic had recently revealed an under-sea range, its highest portion surfacing in the Azores. Donnelly seized on this as evidence for Atlantis, which, he said, was indeed formerly above water over a wide area, the last fragment of an older land-mass. It was the real location of Eden, and the home of a splendid civilization, ancestral to several and senior to all. Its empire spread far in both directions. The civilizations of Egypt and America began as its principal offshoots. The gods and goddesses of mythology were its kings and queens, uncomprehendingly deified.

Donnelly credited his Atlanteans with inventing alphabetic writing and creating or inspiring artworks and monuments on both sides of the ocean. They practised monotheistic sun-worship; early religions elsewhere reflect a decadence from this, following the parent country's submergence. And the submergence itself accounts for all legends of a great Flood. Donnelly's book was a best-seller.

The gateway of the Treasury of Atreus, Mycenae, *c.* 1300 BC: architecture said to show Atlantean influence in Greece.

Corridor of the Palace, Palenque, *c.* 7th century BC: architecture said to show Atlantean influence in southern Mexico.

Portrait of Ignatius Donnelly.

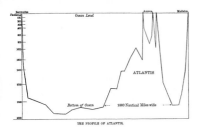

The evolution of alphabets, from Donnelly's
*Atlantis: The Antediluvian World*, 1882.

Sun-worshipping native Americans, supposedly inheritors of Atlantean
religion. Engraving from Théodore de Bry's *America*, 1590.

Donnelly's profile of the Atlantic sea-bed.
The vertical scale is much greater than the
horizontal. From *Atlantis: The Antediluvian
World*, 1882.

Mesopotamian worship of the sun-god implied in Donnelly's scheme
to be a survival of Atlantis's solar monotheism. Tablet from Abu
Habbah, Iraq, *c*. 870 BC.

Aztec drawing of the ancestral migration from
an island to the American continent, cited as
evidence for Atlantean colonization of Mexico.
Part of the Boturini screenfold, *c*. 1168.

# TRANS-OCEANIC ECHOES

How can you prove the reality of a country no longer there? Donnelly employed a method foreshadowed by Helena Petrovna Blavatsky, founder of the Theosophical Society. He instanced parallels between the Old World and the New, and argued that some are close enough to imply a common source in between, namely Atlantis.

One such datum is pre-Christian reverence for the cross as a sacred symbol. Another is the presence of pyramids in Egypt and Mexico, both claimed as Atlantean colonies. Sweden has prehistoric pyramidal monuments, and Sweden too, according to Donnelly, was partly within Atlantis's empire.

A side issue in this discussion is the question of elephants. Plato says Atlantis had many, and so of course has Africa, but the America opened up by Columbus had none. Nevertheless, a few pre-Columbian artworks can be interpreted as depicting them. Perhaps Atlanteans exported them in both directions, but to America only in small numbers, so that the species died out.

The anthropologist Lewis Spence, while rejecting Donnelly's advanced civilization, assembled facts of similar type in support of an Atlantean 'culture-complex' spanning the ocean. They included evidences of ancient witchcraft, and ritual practices such as head-flattening and mummification.

Flattened forehead in North America, as found among the Chinook people. Drawing after George Catlin from Donnelly's *Atlantis: The Antediluvian World*, 1882.

Maya sculpture showing elephant-like profiles and riders wearing turbans. Relief from Stela B, Copan, Honduras, AD 731.

Egyptian heads with flattened foreheads. From *Atlantis: The Antediluvian World*, 1882.

Prehistoric monuments in Sweden, said to be tombs. Woodcut from Olaus Magnus's *Historia de gentibus septentrionalis*, 1555.

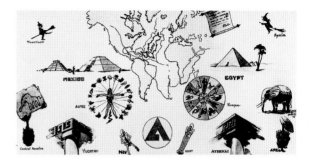

Parallels between the Old and New Worlds, with a map reconstituting a common source between them. Map and symbols from the film *Atlantis, the Lost Continent*, 1961.

Mummy of Tuthmosis III found at Deir el-Bahri, Egypt. Eighteenth Dynasty.

Pyramid of the Sun at Teotihuacán, Mexico, c. 100 BC.

Chac, the Maya rain-god, with a head-dress suggesting an elephant's face and ears. Sculptured head from Stela C, Copan, Honduras, AD 782.

# ATLANTIS'S IMPRINT

/////////////////////////////////////////////////////////////////////////////////////////////////////////////////////////////////////////

Once Atlantean influence is granted, many things can be seen as its products, and as relics and evocations of the lost culture. Massive stonework at Cuzco, in Peru, has been explained as Atlantean. So have the tall statues in Mexico usually ascribed to the pyramid-building Toltecs. A fact that may be urged in favour of such opinions is that pre-Columbian art does offer human images which are not Native American – faces suggesting Africa, and men with European-type features and beards. Though North America has nothing like these, and no pyramids either, it has very large mounds, and the mound-builders too are drawn into the Atlantologists' scheme.

In the Old World, artefacts and sculptures that do not fit acknowledged patterns have been construed similarly. While serious researchers have wondered about the megalithic monuments as a source for the idea of Atlantis, enthusiasts have been much more specific and credited Atlantean colonists with building Stonehenge.

It is not like anything else that has been given such an origin, yet, admittedly, it is unique among megaliths in its architectural style, and its use of stones that are shaped and fitted together. The feeling that it must be due to some mysterious agency is of long standing. Legends far older than Atlantology attribute it to giants, or the wizard Merlin, or the Devil. Even modern archaeologists used to look outside Britain, and postulate experts from Mycenae in Greece, before carbon-dating upset their chronology.

Given an Atlantean Stonehenge, plus the well-known notion of its being a temple of Druids, it was a logical step to represent the Druids themselves as inheritors of Atlantis's Ancient Wisdom.

The great mound at Marietta, Ohio, perhaps a crude form of pyramid. Lithograph after Charles Sullivan from E. G. Squier and E. H. Davis's *Ancient Monuments of the Mississippi Valley*, 1847.

Stonehenge, 2nd millennium BC.

A colossal head with features of negroid type from San Lorenzo, Mexico, suggests the presence of non-Americans long before Columbus. Olmec, 1st millennium BC.

Megalith-building giants in Britain. Engraving from Jan Picardt's *Korte Beschryvinge van eenige verborgene Antiquiteten*, 1660.

An Arch-Druid in judicial robes, as imagined in the 19th century. Lithograph from S. R. Meyrick and C. H. Smith's *The Costume of the Original Inhabitants of the British Isles*, 1815.

Masonry at Cuzco, Peru's principal city in the Inca period. 15th century AD.

III

# REVELATIONS TO COME?

A recurrent feature of ideas about Golden Ages and Ancient Wisdom is a belief that the loss of them is not final: the glory is somehow still extant, at least potentially, and may revive or be reinstated. This takes on a mythic character in such motifs as the immortality and return of King Arthur. But it can also take religious and political forms. In the 16th century Christian reformers appealed to the Church's pristine purity and sought to restore it. And 18th-century French revolutionaries, inspired by Rousseau, asserted the freedom and equality of primitive humankind and aspired to bring it back. Even in science, Isaac Newton (to cite a major example) thought the laws of the universe were known long ago in a wiser age and he was simply rediscovering them.

What then about the lost glories of Atlantis? Can they have been preserved, can they ever be reborn? Novelists such as Dennis Wheatley have imagined a small Atlantean community as never perishing, and surviving in concealment. But Atlantologists, besides alleging inheritors like the Druids, have dwelt on the special role of Egypt as Atlantis's offspring.

Augustus le Plongeon, an early researcher, published an account of a queen of Atlantis who gave Egypt its civilization and became the goddess Isis. Egyptian sun-worship could have retained features of the Atlantean solar cult described by Donnelly. And if Egypt preserved anything at all, it may have preserved more, in secrecy, that will emerge in a future restoration. Two claimants to paranormal enlightenment, H. C. Randall-Stevens and the more famous Edgar Cayce, have spoken of a concealed Hall of Records associated with the Great Pyramid – perhaps under or near the Sphinx. This is a storehouse of Atlantean history and knowledge. Some day it will come to light, and much that is lost will be given to the world again.

The promise of a purified Christianity: John Bunyan's story of the pilgrimage to the Celestial City. Engraved frontispiece and title to Bunyan's *Pilgrim's Progress*, 1693.

An early sectional diagram of the Great Pyramid at Giza, *c*. 2570 BC. Engraving from John Greaves's *Pyramidographia*, 1646.

Regenerated man, imagined during the French Revolution in the spirit of Jean-Jacques Rousseau. Symbolic print by J. L. Perée, 1791.

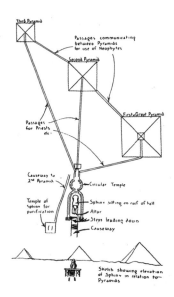

Randall-Stevens's inspirational drawing of the Pyramids and underground Masonic Centre, of Atlantean origin. From *Atlantis to the Latter Days*, 1966.

The Sphinx at Giza, *c.* 2530 BC, believed by Randall-Stevens and Cayce to mark the approximate location of an Atlantean Hall of Records. Lithograph after David Roberts, *c.* 1839.

An offshoot of Atlantis's solar cult? The boat of the Egyptian sun-god crossing the Ocean, symbolized by a snake. Painting from the tomb of Seti I, Thebes, 1318–1301 BC.

Ceremony of the cult of Isis, sometimes interpreted as a migrant queen of Atlantis. Wallpainting from Pompeii, before AD 79.

# OCCULT APPROACHES

Atlantis, as re-evoked by Donnelly, fired many imaginations. For that very reason it posed a fresh problem. Having been told so much, people longed to know more, to verify his reconstruction and give it substance. But how to proceed further? No adequate method of diving had been invented, and while soundings could trace the sea-bed's contours, they revealed little of what was on it. Investigation, seemingly, could be pursued in only two ways: by finding other accounts of Atlantis, and by occult or paranormal techniques.

Both methods were pioneered by Theosophy. Its exponent Madame Blavatsky, who had anticipated Donnelly to a slight extent, published what she asserted to be secret texts, fitting the Atlanteans into a series of 'root-races' divided into sub-races and covering millions of years. The details, however, were too strange and cryptic for the general public. It was left to a follower, William Scott-Elliot, to fill in Atlantis's history comprehensibly. He did it by 'astral clairvoyance'.

Scott-Elliot combined Blavatsky's racial scheme with Donnelly's picture of Atlantis as the prime source of civilization. It appeared, though, that not all Atlanteans counted in that respect. He identified those who principally did as a sub-race whom he called Toltecs. To their more orthodox achievements he added magical powers. His Toltec-dominated Atlantis had an Ancient Wisdom of its own that was largely lost in the inundation, and never recovered.

He brought back Plato's conception of the collapse as more than accidental. Plato made it – or, to be precise, manifestly intended to make it – a divine judgment on overweening imperialism. Scott-Elliot laid the blame on unhallowed sorcery. Henceforth, nemesis through misuse of power (of one kind or another) was restored to the Atlantis myth in its exploitation by various writers.

*The Unfed Light in the Atlantean Chapel:* a picture inspired by the 'Phylos' communications of Frederick Spencer Oliver. From Phylos's [Oliver's] *An Earth Dweller's Return,* 1970.

Blavatsky cited dragons as evidence for humanity's great antiquity, on the ground that they were dinosaurs. Engraving from Athanasius Kircher's *Mundus subterraneus*, 1678.

An occult reconstruction of an Atlantean city. From Colin Amery's *New Atlantis*, 1976.

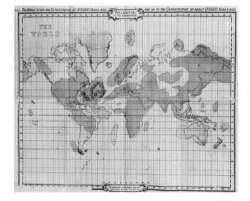

A world map drawn by William Scott-Elliot illustrating his revelations about lost lands in the distant Theosophical past.

Australian aborigines, also of reputedly Lemurian ancestry. Engraving from D. Collins's *Account of the English Colony in New South Wales*, 1798.

Bushwoman and child from the Kaukau Veldt, descendants, according to Scott-Elliot, of a 'Lemurian' race from which Atlanteans too evolved.

# LEMURIA AND MU

When the new version of Atlantis grew popular, the kind of thinking which it fostered produced an alternative. Another Atlantis, even a sort of rival, began to stir.

Some years previously a zoologist had argued that a land-bridge must once have spanned the Indian Ocean, because of the distribution of certain animals. Among these were lemurs, so he dubbed the sunken country 'Lemuria'. Madame Blavatsky adopted and extended it, taking it round into the Atlantic and far across the Pacific, and making it the home of her third root-race, prior to the Atlanteans. Scott-Elliot followed up. He had a low opinion of the Lemurians, who were not properly human at all, and only made what progress they did through extra-terrestrial aid.

Their status was transformed by Colonel James Churchward. A Maya text, the *Troano Codex*, had been translated as an account of the destruction of a country called Mu. At first Mu was assumed to be Atlantis, but Churchward placed it in the Pacific. It was not the same as the Theosophists' huge Lemuria, but was the principal portion of it. He said a series of stone tablets in an Indian temple, written in 'Naacal', told its story. Mu, not Donnelly's Atlantis, was the location of Eden and the first great civilization, superior to all later ones. Religious symbols in many places are of Muvian inspiration and attest its reality. Volcanic action broke it up, but it survives, atomized, as Polynesia.

Believers in Mu or Lemuria – now virtually identified – have claimed Easter Island with its strange statues as evidence. According to some, the west-coast region of the United States is part of Lemuria, attached to another continent.

A longboat of Muror (the name given to Mu, otherwise Lemuria, by Tony Earll) from Earll's *Mu Revealed*, 1970.

One of the volcanic eruptions that destroyed Mu. Drawing by Churchward from his *Lost Continent of Mu*, 1931.

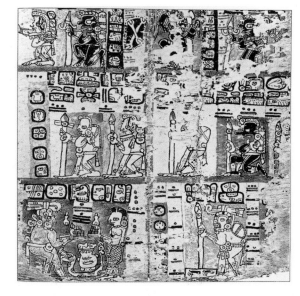

Cruciform design, a Muvian symbol of creation; and Mu's cosmogonic diagram said to be paralleled in various contexts. From Churchward's *The Sacred Symbols of Mu*, 1933.

Part of the Maya *Troano Codex*. Facsimile, 1930.

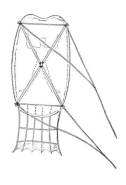

Symbolic figure of Mu as world-ruler. Bronze statue from Uighur, Central Asia, said to be 18,000 years old. From Churchward's *The Sacred Symbols of Mu*, 1933.

A flying-machine in Atlantis by Léon Krier, 1987.

A 'Murovian' man-lifting kite, perhaps ancestral to the Atlantean flying-machine. From Earll's *Mu Revealed*, 1970.

# SHASTA: A LEMURIAN COLONY

Mount Shasta, in northern California, has a powerful role in Native American myth. The Great Spirit created it first and built the world around it, but without humans. Grizzly bears were to be the ruling species. His primordial grizzlies walked upright and had a language. He hollowed out a space inside Shasta and lived in it. But his daughter ventured into the open and mated with a grizzly. Their offspring were human, and that is how humanity started. Her father emerged, angrily reduced all grizzlies to animal status, retired into the mountain with his daughter, and is still inside.

The mystique of lost lands began to focus on Shasta in a book published in 1894, *A Dweller on Two Planets*. Its author Frederick Spencer Oliver, who lived near the mountain, explained that the story had been communicated to him by 'Phylos the Thibetan'. Most of it is set in Atlantis, but Oliver also speaks of Lemuria and a subterranean temple in Mount Shasta. He may or may not have known the native myth; Donnelly certainly did.

Readers impressed by the book have taken it seriously and expanded its message, speaking of a stone door in the mountain and a passage leading to a whole underground realm. Lemurian 'adepts' are in there, it is said, and occasionally come out. They have been sighted performing rituals, dressed in long robes.

The Harmonic Convergence in 1987, a New Age event, attracted thousands to the mountain. Its aura has inspired a group of artists, the New Visionaries. While sacred mountains are numerous, only a minority claim inhabited interiors as Shasta does. Glastonbury Tor, another centre of the Harmonic Convergence, is a British instance with a mythic background that may be thousands of years old. Its reputed occupant is Gwyn, king of the fairy-folk and the underworld, a former Celtic god.

*The Sacred Mountain* by Paul Gauguin, 1892.

Glastonbury Tor in Somerset, said, like Mount Shasta, to be hollow and to house mysterious beings.

*The Hermit of Mount Shasta* by Cheryl Yambrach Rose, 1987.

Astral Cathedral over the Inner Temple, Mount Shasta. Lithograph drawing by Teodors A. Liliensteins from Earlyne Chaney's *Secrets of Mount Shasta*, 1953.

The 'Chinese Master' before the great stone door leading to the Lemurian retreat inside Mount Shasta. From Phylos's [Frederick Spencer Oliver's] *An Earth Dweller's Return*, 1970.

# LUNAR UPHEAVALS AND HIDDEN SPACES

Atlantologists have made few converts of academic standing. In the eyes of official history and official science, Atlantis remains a 'fringe' subject. Significantly, it is involved with other 'fringe' subjects. Speculative minds unawed by orthodoxy, and attracted by one such topic, are apt to be attracted by others and to trace connections.

Atlantis was drawn, for instance, into the cosmology of Hans Höbiger. According to this, Earth has had a whole series of satellites, at varying distances. The moon before the present one spiralled closer as its orbit decayed. Its upward gravitational pull caused earthquakes, eruptions, and monstrous tides. Atlantis – two Atlantises, in fact – fell victim to this lunar vagary and others.

The wish to believe that the lost land is not entirely lost, that descendants of its brilliant people are living still and may be active, has involved it both with the Hollow Earth theory and with Unidentified Flying Objects. The former has a long pedigree. Notions of mysterious underground realms, abodes of gods or fairy-folk or superior beings, have existed from time immemorial. A subterranean romance called *The Coming Race* (1871), by the Victorian occultist Bulwer-Lytton, was taken seriously by many readers. Atlantis has a place in this kind of imagining. Its fictitious survivors in Dennis Wheatley's novel inhabit a cavity below the Azores. The mystique of Mount Shasta is a Lemurian counterpart.

An extreme, quasi-scientific, hypothesis – likewise used by fantasy writers – goes much further. It alleges that this planet is hollow more or less as a football is hollow, with an interior world. Its advocates have spoken of entrances at the poles. Inhabitants, who may be Atlanteans, live inside; and these perhaps are responsible for UFOs, dispatched into the outer atmosphere on undisclosed missions that may include bringing back surface-dwellers.

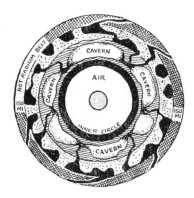

Inner-earth caverns and geological infrastructure. From Colin Amery's *New Atlantis*, 1976.

A section of the earth's interior, showing the polar entrance to a hypothetical inner Atlantis. From William Reed's *Phantom of the Poles*, 1906.

The arrival of the spacecraft from the film *Close Encounters of the Third Kind*, 1977.

The doorway to an underground temple of Eternal Wisdom. Engraving from Heinrich Khunrath's *Amphitheatrum sapientiae aeternae*, 1602.

Travis Walton's abduction by a UFO. According to one theory, they are sent by Atlanteans from inside the earth. From *Official UFO* magazine, July 1976.

# THE PLACE OF QUIETUDE

Madame Blavatsky and, to a greater extent, the breakaway Theosophist Alice Bailey, took up a belief of Lamaistic Buddhism in Tibet and Mongolia: a belief about a place called Shambhala. Its name means 'quietude' or 'bliss' and it supplied the main hint for James Hilton's Shangri-la in *Lost Horizon*. Unlike Shangri-la, however, it lies concealed in an ill-defined north. It is a paradisal abode of Ancient Wisdom. Theosophical Lemurians and Atlanteans are said to have settled there, or in the near neighbourhood. Shambhala has thus been made a point of convergence for the occult histories of both the lost lands.

The Theosophical Shambhala is, or was, in the Gobi Desert. If it still exists, it is 'etheric' and imperceptible to the uninitiated. But the Gobi location has no support from authentic Buddhist tradition. Researches by the artist and anthropologist Nicholas Roerich (himself a Theosophist for a while, but after his own fashion) point to the Altai Mountains, which sweep around from Mongolia into Siberia, and especially to their highest peak, Mount Belukha – immemorially revered as a Dwelling of Gods.

Independently of any of this, the 18th-century astronomer Jean Sylvain Bailly believed there was evidence for an ancient centre of science in the Altai–Baikal area. He even involved his claim with a theory that Spitzbergen (formerly warmer) was the real Atlantis, and that Atlanteans migrated south towards the Altai. Serious reasons exist for suspecting that the Altai–Baikal area actually was a cultural seed-bed during several millennia BC, and the Shambhala tradition may relate to that. If so, Bailly's conjecture was extraordinarily acute, and Madame Blavatsky and Alice Bailey were right to pick on Shambhala as significant. These quite separate attempts to find traces of Atlantis appear, however puzzlingly, to have led where there is something to be found.

*Shambhala* by Rodney Birkett, one of the New Visionary group associated with Mount Shasta.

A forced landing in Shangri-la. James Hilton's version of Shambhala in *Lost Horizon*, 1937, has been speculatively connected with both Lemuria and Atlantis.

Nicholas Roerich in Mongolia, 1927, holding the banner symbolic of Shambhala.

An alchemical symbolic picture distantly parallels Shambhala as an earthly point of contact with higher realms. Woodcut from 1678.

Rudrachakrin, the king of Shambhala in the Buddhist tradition. Tibetan Tanka painting, late 18th to early 19th century.

*Treasures of the Mountain* by Nicholas Roerich (1874–1947).

# REALIZATIONS

Atlantis has figured in novels, films, poems and operas. Jules Verne's Captain Nemo is the first of several fictional rediscoverers. Arthur Conan Doyle's story *The Maracot Deep* (1929) combines science with the revelations of Scott-Elliot. Other novelists, notably Cutcliffe Hyne, have gone back into the past and imagined Atlantis as it might have been when above water.

An early French film, *L'Atlantide*, popularized a theory shifting it to the Sahara. Later films have kept Plato's location. One low-budget oddity, *Fire Maidens from Outer Space* (1956), took astronauts to a moon of Jupiter where they met descendants of Atlanteans who escaped from the disaster. The technological implications, surely the most remarkable in any treatment, remained undeveloped.

Augustus le Plongeon, the investigator who said Isis was an Atlantean queen, had a wife who transposed his ideas into narrative verse. She was an indifferent poet. Of more literary value is an epic in Catalan by Jacinto Verdaguer. Manuel de Falla, the Spanish composer of *The Three-Cornered Hat*, based an opera on this – for concert performance rather than the theatre. Another opera, in a lighter vein, is Sir Gerald Hargreaves's 'fantasy with music' *Atalanta*, exceptional among modern works in maintaining contact with Plato's original story.

The lost land has found its way into comic books and graphic novels. *Indiana Jones and the Fate of Atlantis* embodied a real study of Plato, even mentioning orichalcum.

Despite this varied output, Atlantis cannot be said to have inspired a modern work of unquestionable stature in any medium. Perhaps that is still to come.

The Temple of Poseidon. Set design by Sir Gerald Hargreaves for his opera *Atalanta, c.* 1950.

A wise man instructing the hero of Edgar Rice Burroughs's *Princess of Mars*, 1917, which transplants the Atlantean conceptions of Theosophists to another planet.

The queen of Atlantis located in the Sahara. A scene from the film *L'Atlantide*, 1921, based on Pierre Benoit's novel.

The chief city of Atlantis from the film *Atlantis, the Lost Continent*, 1961.

A piazza in Atlantis. Drawing for an architectural scheme by Léon Krier, 1987.

Indiana Jones uses orichalcum, a rare metal mentioned by Plato, to open the door to Atlantis. From Dan Barry and William Messner-Loebs's *Indiana Jones and the Fate of Atlantis*, 1991.

ALDER, VERA STANLEY, *The Initiation of the World*, London, 1969

AMERY, COLIN, *New Atlantis: the Secret of the Sphinx*, London, 1976

ASHE, GEOFFREY, *Dawn Behind the Dawn*, New York, 1992

——, *Land to the West*, London, 1962

BACON, FRANCIS, *The Advancement of Learning and New Atlantis*, Oxford, 1974

BERLITZ, CHARLES, *The Mystery of Atlantis*, New York, 1969

BERNBAUM, EDWIN, *The Way to Shambhala*, Los Angeles, 1989

BLAVATSKY, H. P., *Isis Unveiled*, 2 vols, Pasadena, Calif., 1972

——, *The Secret Doctrine*, 2 vols, Pasadena, Calif., 1970

BRAMWELL, JAMES, *Lost Atlantis*, London, 1937

CERVÉ, W. S., *Lemuria: the Lost Continent of the Pacific*, San José, Calif., 1931

CHURCHWARD, JAMES, *The Children of Mu*, London, 1931

——, *The Sacred Symbols of Mu*, New York, 1933

DAMON, S. FOSTER, *A Blake Dictionary*, New York, 1971

DE CAMP, L. SPRAGUE, and CATHERINE C. DE CAMP, *Citadels of Mystery*, London, 1972

DONNELLY, IGNATIUS, *Atlantis: the Antediluvian World*, ed. and rev. Egerton Sykes, New York, 1949

EARLL, TONY, *Mu Revealed*, New York, 1970

GRAVES, ROBERT, *The Greek Myths*, 2 vols, Harmondsworth, 1960

LE POER TRENCH, BRINSLEY, *Operation Earth*, London, 1969

——, *Temple of the Stars*, London, 1962

LEVY, JOEL, *The Atlas of Atlantis and Other Lost Civilizations*, London, 2007

LUCE, J. V., *The End of Atlantis*, London, 1969

MEREZHKOVSKY, DIMITRI, *Atlantis/Europe: the Secret of the West*, Blauvelt, N.Y., 1971

MICHELL, JOHN, *The View Over Atlantis*, London, 1972

——, *The New View Over Atlantis*, London, 1986

'PHYLOS THE THIBETAN' (F. S. OLIVER), *A Dweller on Two Planets*, London 1970

——, *An Earth Dweller's Return*, Alhambra, Calif.,1969

PLATO, *Timaeus and Critias*, trans. R. G. Bury, in Works, Loeb Classical Library, vol. 7, London and New York, 1929

RANDALL-STEVENS, H. C., *Atlantis to the Latter Days*, Jersey, 1966

SCOTT-ELLIOT, W., *The Story of Atlantis and The Lost Lemuria* (two books combined), London, 1962

SMITH, WARREN, *This Hollow Earth*, London, 1977

SPANUTH, JÜRGEN, *Atlantis – the Mystery Unravelled*, London, 1956

SPENCE, LEWIS, *Atlantis in America*, London, 1925

——, *The History of Atlantis*, London, 1926

——, *The Problem of Atlantis*, London, 1924

STEIGER, BRAD, *Atlantis Rising*, New York, 1973

TIME-LIFE BOOKS, *Mysterious Lands and Peoples*, Alexandria, Va., 1991

——, *Mystic Places*, Alexandria, Va., 1987

TOMAS, ANDREW, *Atlantis: From Legend to Discovery*, London, 1973

ZANGGER, EBERHARD, *The Flood from Heaven*, London, 1992

# ACKNOWLEDGMENTS

*Numbers refer to page numbers.*

a=above, c=centre, b=below, l=left, r=right

*The objects and illustrations reproduced are in the following collections:*

Athens: ARCHAEOLOGICAL MUSEUM 97al | Berlin: STAATLICHE MUSEEN 97br | Chantilly: MUSÉE CONDÉ 105bl | HOLKHAM HALL, Norfolk 42 | Istanbul: ARCHAEOLOGICAL MUSEUMS 99cr | Kaunas: ČIURLIONIS ART GALLERY 41, 90, 100r | PRENTENKABINET, Rijksuniversiteit te Leiden 100l | London: BRITISH MUSEUM 101bl, 101br, 107br, 117ar; SIR JOHN SOANE'S MUSEUM 65; TATE GALLERY 99cl | Madrid: MUSEO NACIONAL DEL PRADO 7, 11 | Minneapolis: UNIVERSITY OF MINNESOTA, James Ford Bell Library 74 | Munich: BAYERISCHE STAATSGEMÄLDESAMMLUNGEN, Alte Pinakothek 72; NEUE PINAKOTHEK 99br | LANDESMUSEUM MÜNSTER, Sammlung Cremer 85 | BIBLIOTHÈQUE DE NAMUR 82 | Naples: MUSEO NAZIONALE 133br | THE HISTORIC NEW ORLEANS COLLECTION, Museum/Research Center (acc. no. 1974.25.19.640a) 22 | New York: THE RARE BOOK AND MANUSCRIPT LIBRARY, Columbia University Libraries 25; FRICK COLLECTION 54; THE METROPOLITAN MUSEUM OF ART 101al, Gift of Samuel P. Avery Jr., 1904 69; THE NEW-YORK HISTORICAL SOCIETY 80–81 | NICHOLAS ROERICH MUSEUM 30, 123al, 123br | Paris: MUSÉE DU LOUVRE 8, 99tr; Musée Guimet 29 | Oxford: ASHMOLEAN MUSEUM, 99bl | PHILADELPHIA MUSEUM OF ART 118l | PRIVATE COLLECTION 78 | PRIVATE COLLECTION/BRIDGEMAN ART LIBRARY, London 18 | Rome: VATICAN 16592, PIPILI 34 #92 961 | Seville: MUSEO ARQUEOLÓGICO PROVINCIAL 60 | Sousse: MUSÉE ARCHÉOLOGIQUE 99tl | MUSEO REGIONAL DE VERACRUZ, Mexico 111al | VIRGINIA MUSEUM OF FINE ARTS, Richmond. GIFT OF SHOJI YAMANAKA IN MEMORY OF ALAN PRIEST 123bl | Washington, D.C.: LIBRARY OF CONGRESS 87 | WORCESTER ART MUSEUM, Massachusetts/BRIDGEMAN ART LIBRARY, London 14 | ZÜRICH-KÜSNACHT, Sammlung Augusto Cansser 31.

*Sources of photographs:*

AKG-IMAGES 49, 53, 96r | ALINARI 13, 47 | ARTOTHEK 72 | PETER BELLWOOD 111br | Courtesy of RODNEY BIRKETT 122bl | ERNA & HELMUT BLENCK 115br | JANET and COLIN BORD 118br | THE BRITISH FILM INSTITUTE, London 19, 109ar, 121a, 122br, 125al, 125ar | THE BRITISH TOURIST BOARD 111ar | ORIENTAL INSTITUTE OF THE UNIVERSITY OF CHICAGO 103b | CHRISTIE'S, London 104br | Cologne: FORSCHUNGSARCHIV FÜR RÖMISCHE PLASTIK, Universität zu Köln 42 | COUNTRYWIDE PUBLICATIONS 121br | Drawing by F. DAVALOS 111al | GIRAUDON 105bl | IRMGARD GROTH-KIMBALL 106c | PRIVATE COLLECTION. Colorphoto HANS HINZ 78 | HIRMER FOTOARCHIV 46, 66–67 | E. K. KING (Lord Kingsborough), Antiquities of Mexico (London 1830–48) 107bl | LÉON KRIER 89, 117bc, 125br | MARY EVANS PICTURE LIBRARY 116br | © RICHARD MASCHMEYER/ALAMY 26 | After A. MAUDSLAY, Biologia Centrali-Americana (London, 1889) 108al | MINNESOTA HISTORICAL SOCIETY, St Paul 106br | ALPHONSE DE NEUVILLE in *Vingt Mille lieues sous les mers* by Jules Verne, Éditions Hetzel (1896) 83 | NEW YORK AMERICAN (1912) 97bl | H. RECK, *Santorin: Der Werdegang eines Inselvulkans und sein Ausbruch 1925–28* (Berlin, 1936) 102bl | © LEE ROBINSON/ALAMY 21 | CHERYL YAMBRACH ROSE 35, 119al | J. A. SABLOFF 109bl | EDWIN SMITH 71, 106bl | G. E. SMITH, The Royal Mummies (Cairo, 1912) 109al | Courtesy of the THEOSOPHICAL SOCIETY OF ENGLAND 17, 18 | JULES VERNE, *Vingt Mille lieues sous les mers*, Éditions Hetzel (1870) 85 | VOLCANIC FILMS LTD 38.

# INDEX

Page numbers in *italic* refer to illustrations.